THE DIVIDED FLAME

Other Books by Howard A. Snyder . . .

The Community of the King

A Kingdom Manifesto

Liberating the Church: The Ecology of Church and Kingdom

One Hundred Years at Spring Arbor

The Problem of Wineskins: Church Structure in a Technological Age

The Radical Wesley and Patterns for Church Renewal

Other Books by Daniel V. Runyon . . .

The No-Diet Fitness Book

Administrator's Guide to Feelin' Good (Co-author)

THE DIVIDED FLAME

WESLEYANS AND THE
CHARISMATIC RENEWAL

Howard A. Snyder

with Daniel V. Runyon

FRANCIS ASBURY PRESS
of Zondervan Publishing House
Grand Rapids, Michigan

THE DIVIDED FLAME: WESLEYANS AND THE CHARISMATIC RENEWAL
Copyright © 1986 by Howard A. Snyder

FRANCIS ASBURY PRESS is an imprint of Zondervan Publishing House, 1415 Lake Drive, S.E., Grand Rapids, Michigan 49506.

Library of Congress Cataloging in Publication Data

Snyder, Howard A.
    The divided flame.

    Bibliography: p.
    Includes index.
    1. Holiness churches. 2. Pentecostalism. 3. Holiness churches—Relations—Pentecostal churches. 4. Pentecostal churches—Relations—Holiness churches. I. Runyon, Daniel V. II. Title.
BX7990.H6S69   1986   287   86-3548
ISBN 0310-75181-0

Edited by James E. Ruark
Designed by Louise Bauer

Printed in the United States of America

87   88   89   90   91   92   93   94 / 10   9   8   7   6   5   4   3   2

CONTENTS

INTRODUCTION

Words make a difference. Words like "holiness," "pentecostal," and "charismatic" have sometimes been fighting words. But they can also serve as bridges to broader understanding.

The word "charismatic" serves the contemporary Charismatic Movement as "holiness" did John Wesley's most lively descendants in the nineteenth century. Key words and concepts like these embody the organizing center of a movement. Because of this, "charismatic"— like "holiness" and "pentecostal"—quickly becomes a slippery word, meaning different things to different people. Like so many terms with a biblical base, however, it is too good a word to be abandoned because of differing meanings and connotations. In banning the word we may also close the door to important truth or restrict the free flow of the Holy Spirit among us.

Anyone who feels that the word "charismatic" is too tainted or loaded to be useful today might consider such biblical terms as "presbyterian," "episcopal," "baptist," and "ecumenical." Like "charismatic," these words come directly from New Testament Greek. Their modern English connotations don't warrant dropping such words from our vocabulary. Rather, we should rediscover and reaffirm their true biblical significance. We should watch for meanings we may be missing.

It is fully appropriate, therefore, for Wesleyans to have dialogue with Charismatic Christianity. By "Charismatic Christianity" we mean primarily the contemporary Charismatic Movement in its various forms and secondarily its Pentecostal antecedents. Despite the increasing awareness of common Charismatic, Pentecostal, and Holiness roots in the Wesleyan Revival, to date little dialogue has developed between contemporary Wesleyans and Charismatics. Such dialogue is needed today.

In this book we hope to show that Wesleyans have both something to learn from and something to say to contemporary Charismatics. We also want to recognize that God is using the Charismatic Movement today. To recognize this is a thoroughly Wesleyan attitude.

How does a Wesleyan dialogue with Charismatic Christianity? Rather than comparing our theology or practice point by point, we have chosen to address the *central question* that Charismatic Christianity raises for us: *In what sense is Christian experience, or the church, charismatic?* If the Charismatic Movement raises valid biblical questions for us—and it does—then it is more important to deal with those questions than merely to catalog the pluses or minuses of the movement.

First we must investigate the question of the charismatic nature of the church. Then we will ask whether Wesleyanism is a charismatic movement, examining Wesley's theology and the Methodist and Holiness movements in the light of Scripture. Finally we will comment on Wesleyan and Charismatic Christianity today and offer some suggestions in the direction of a biblical Wesleyan ecclesiology—since the charismatic emphasis inevitably raises the question of church structure and practice.

While this book is not primarily an historical study, we have supplied enough historical perspective (we trust) to make our theological and practical analyses intelligible.

In John 17 Jesus prayed that the church might be one so that the world would know him. This prayer excludes neither Wesleyan nor Charismatic believers. It is our conviction that Jesus was more concerned about the unity of the church than most Christians are today. Our hope is that this book may lead to greater unity among believers, thereby advancing the cause of Christ, the church, and the kingdom.

Howard A. Snyder
Chicago, Illinois

Daniel V. Runyon
Spring Arbor, Michigan

1

IS THE CHURCH CHARISMATIC?

In the biblical understanding of the term, is the church charismatic? Some flatly say so. W. T. Purkiser affirms, "In the New Testament use of the term, all Christians are charismatic."[1] But if to be Christian is to be charismatic, what does the word mean?

THE MEANINGS OF CHARISMATIC

In the popular mind "charismatic" is almost universally linked with tongues-speaking. Only in very recent years, as the Charismatic Movement has matured and assumed varying forms, has that association begun to break down.

There are, of course, other associations to the term. We may distinguish three main meanings in popular usage: the sociological, the religious, and the biblical.[2]

The *sociological meaning* traces back to the German sociologist Max Weber and is commonly expressed today in reference to a "charismatic leader." Whether active politically or religiously, this person exhibits a personal magnetism more or less independent of official status or position. While this meaning distorts the biblical origin of the word "charismatic," it ultimately springs from that source.

The *popular religious meaning* is also a distortion of the biblical basis, both because of its almost universal association with tongues and because of the related notion that charismatic gifts are always dramatic and in some sense ecstatic or undisciplined. There is, however, an important biblical meaning of "charismatic." The popular sociological and religious uses make it difficult for us to understand the root meaning of the term and compel us to go to Scripture with our questions.

THE BIBLICAL MEANING

The word "charismatic" derives from the Greek word *charisma*, "grace gift," and finally from *charis*, "grace." A related word is the verb *charidzomai*, "to give freely or graciously as a favor."

These words bring us to the heart of the gospel. "For it is by grace [*charis*] you have been saved," Paul writes in Ephesians 2:8–9, "through faith—and this not from yourselves, it is the gift of God—not by works, so that no one can boast." God is graciously self-giving. His mercy and grace toward us as sinners and toward the Church are the foundation for the life of the Christian community.

This truth comes through clearly in several of the instances of *charidzomai* in the New Testament. For example, Romans 8:32: "He who did not spare his own Son, but gave him up for us all—how will he not also, along with him, graciously give [*charisetai*] us all things?" God's gift of his own Son is the supreme manifestation of his grace and assures us that in Christ we will be given "all things" necessary to full Christian life and experience.

Paul frequently underscores the fact that salvation is a gracious gift, not a matter of works or law. So he argues in Galatians 3:18, "For if the inheritance depends on the law, then it no longer depends on a promise; but God *in his grace gave* [*kecharistai*] it to Abraham through a promise." Like Abraham, the people of God today are justified and live on the basis of a gracious promise.[3]

Therefore the church is charismatic in this fundamental sense. It is formed and lives by God's grace. It has received the gift of God, which is salvation through Jesus Christ. The gift is, in fact, Jesus Christ himself—and therefore the Holy Spirit himself. Biblically, this is the indispensable foundation for dealing with the question of the *charismata* ("grace gifts," the plural of *charisma*). God's primary gift is not an "it," a thing, or even a status or position. God's gift is a *Person* and a living, healing *relationship* with that divine Person.

But it is not enough simply to accept the word "charismatic" in this redefined and more basic sense. We must go on to ask how the *gifts* of the Spirit mentioned in the New Testament relate to the fact of the *gift* of the Spirit, of salvation by grace through faith. For the church is also charismatic in the sense that God has apportioned a special measure of grace and giftedness to each believer (Eph. 4:7–8). God promises and gives gifts of the Holy Spirit to build up the church. This is consistent with the gracious work of the same Spirit in regeneration and sanctification.

This perspective underlies the familiar Pauline passages on the *charismata* (Rom. 12:4–8; 1 Cor. 12–14; Eph. 4:7–16) and related passages such as Hebrews 2:4 and 1 Peter 4:10–11. Ephesians 4 indicates that the unity and oneness of the church (4:3–6) are balanced by the diversity and mutuality of its members as a gifted, charismatic community (4:7–16). This understanding of the *charismata* is basic to Paul's whole concept of the church as an organism created and sustained by the grace of God.

An examination of Ephesians 3:2–11 underscores this point and shows how closely *charis* and *charisma* were linked in Paul's thought. Paul says that his hearers know of the "administration" or "economy" (*oikonomia*) of God's grace (*charis*) that had been given him (3:2).

Paul was given a special understanding of God's grace and a commission to reveal and proclaim this to the church and especially to the Gentiles. In verse 7 he says, "I became a servant of this gospel by the gift of God's grace given me through the working of his power." Paul's phrase here is *dōrean tēs charitos*—literally, "gift of the grace" of God—rather than *charisma*. Still, the meaning is clear: Paul himself had received a special charism, a gift of grace, to proclaim the full meaning of the gospel. In verse 8 Paul says that "this grace [*charis*] was given me to preach to the Gentiles the unsearchable riches of Christ." Here he substitutes the word "grace" for "gift of grace." For Paul, the *charismata* and God's grace were so intimately associated that he could sometimes use *charis* in the sense of *charisma*.

Thus Paul saw his own ministry in charismatic terms. We know he was very conscious of his apostleship, and further that he considered apostleship one of the *charismata*—in fact, as the preeminent charismatic gift (1 Cor. 12:28; Eph. 4:11). His description of his own ministry as "grace" and "gift of grace" underscores the fact that Paul understood his own apostleship in charismatic terms.

We see here also that Paul uses "grace" in two distinctive senses. In Ephesians 2:8–9 he refers to the grace of salvation, God's gift through Christ by which we are saved. But in Ephesians 3:8 and 4:7 "grace" is synonymous with *charisma,* that is, "spiritual gift." Thus in Ephesians 4:7 Paul says, "To each one of us grace has been given as Christ apportioned it," and goes on to speak of spiritual gifts. This distributing or apportioning of God's grace to individual believers for edification and ministry is basic to the discussion of 1 Corinthians 12, especially verses 4–7, and reminds us of the reference to "distributions of the Holy Spirit" in Hebrews 2:4.

Note the progression of Paul's thought in Ephesians 4:1–7. You have already been saved by God's grace, and so made one, he says. But within this unity is diversity. Grace has been given not only for your salvation, but also in the form of special endowment to enable each believer to be a useful, functioning member of the Body of Christ. What follows, logically, is a discussion of the gifts of the Spirit.

Therefore the church is charismatic in these two senses. Fundamentally, it is charismatic in that it is called into being and constituted by God's gracious work of salvation effected by the Holy Spirit through faith in Jesus Christ. Secondly, it is charismatic in that God by his Spirit works graciously in the church to build up and equip it for ministry through the distribution of a variety of spiritual gifts.

Several truths follow from this perspective. First, spiritual gifts are not a peripheral or unimportant aspect of the church's life, but are linked to God's gracious action in the events of salvation. Second, this perspective underscores the ecclesiological importance of spiritual gifts. Gifts are not given for private spiritual enjoyment only, but for building up the Christian community. Conversely, gifts are not only a matter of the corporate life of the church but are a very real part of personal Christian experience. In fact, both sanctification and spiritual gifts have this in common: Individual Christian experience builds up the Body, and the church nurtures the lives and ministries of individual believers through the building of a charismatic, sanctifying community. This is the meaning of Ephesians 4:1–16.

In this sense both Christian experience and the church are charismatic. Christian experience is the experience of God's grace in the life of the Christian community.

What, then, is the primary meaning of "charismatic"? We see that biblically the term applies first of all *to the church*, the community of believers, and only secondarily to the believer as an individual. Biblically, "charismatic" describes what the church is like.

By way of summary, and to set the stage for the discussion in later chapters, we may identify four aspects of the charismatic nature of the church. These four points constitute a kind of model of what "charismatic" means in this book and provide the perspective for discussing "the charismatic question" as it applies to our churches today.

1. *The church exists and lives by God's grace* (charis). The church is the special sphere and evidence of God's working graciously by his Spirit to convert, sanctify, equip, and minister through believers "to the praise of his glorious grace" (Eph. 1:6). The church is charismatic because it is fundamentally a grace-endowed organism, not a legal or primarily institutional structure.

2. *The church lives and functions by the action of the Holy Spirit and the distribution of the Spirit's gifts.* The charismatic nature of the church underscores the importance of the Holy Spirit's endowment of believers with his gifts. The work of the Spirit is, of course, much broader than the distribution of gifts, as Wesleyans are quick to point out; but one cannot omit or downplay the role of spiritual gifts without doing violence to the New Testament.

3. *The charismatic emphasis focuses attention on the church as community.* The church was meant to be an intimate community of mutually dependent believers who together make up Christ's Body. But this *koinonia* is often lost due to the gradual drift toward institutionalism that seems to plague all churches, including those in the Holiness tradition. Decline in the knowledge and use of spiritual gifts often goes hand in hand with a decline in *koinonia*. Similarly, recovery of a balanced biblical emphasis on the *charismata* tends to deepen the awareness and

experience of true Christian community. It is no accident that many branches of the Charismatic Movement have led the way in the recovery of a deeper level of Christian community. Many believers who have been attracted to the Charismatic Movement were initially drawn less by the emphasis on tongues or other gifts than by the caring, mutual love, and community that they found among "Charismatics."

4. Finally, *the charismatic emphasis implies some inevitable tension with institutional expressions of the church.* The tension between Spirit and structure is ever present in the life of the church (unless all life has vanished!), as the Wesleyan and Holiness movements can well testify.[4] This does not mean, of course, that every "Charismatic" manifestation is necessarily of the Spirit or that institutional structures are wrong. It does suggest that whenever the Spirit moves in the church, tension will arise between "wine" and "wineskins." The very immediacy of the work of the Spirit in human experience produces tensions with established patterns of life and order.

Study Questions

1. How have you usually understood the word "charismatic"? What kind of emotional response did you experience when you heard this word used?

2. The word "charismatic" is almost universally linked with the practice of tongues-speaking, even though in the Bible this word refers to many gifts of grace. Has this misunderstanding influenced your beliefs about the importance of the various gifts of the Spirit, or gifts of grace? How?

3. Think about the idea of Jesus as a "charismatic leader." In what sense might the life and ministry of Jesus be considered a gift of grace?

4. To what extent does your own church use or exercise the gifts of grace? How crucial are these gifts to the survival and effective ministry of your church?

5. Is your church "charismatic"? In what sense?

2

SPIRITUAL GIFTS FROM THE APOSTLES TO WESLEY

If the church is charismatic biblically, what sort of picture does church history give us? A brief examination of the church in history will set the stage for the questions we face today. First, however, we need to say a word about glossolalia, or speaking in tongues, to explain our approach to the historical issues.

Controversy over charismatic gifts understandably centers most often in the more dramatic manifestations of the Spirit—particularly tongues-speaking, miracles, and healing. This has been true down through history and at present, just as apparently it was at Corinth in the first century. While we rightly insist (with Paul in 1 Corinthians 12–14, for example) that all gifts must be viewed corporately and in the context of love, yet the question always arises: Yes, but what about tongues? Of necessity, therefore, we must give particular attention to glossolalia in the course of this book.

As we will see, it is this gift more than any other that has been the bone of contention between Wesleyan and Pentecostal-Charismatic branches of the church. We therefore briefly trace the history of tongues-speaking in the church, since this is essential for putting the contemporary scene in perspective. But we remind both ourselves and the reader that even this focus runs the risk of distorting the more holistic view of the church as charismatic for which we are arguing.

Two questions invariably arise in discussions of glossolalia: Has tongues-speaking been a rare, only occasional phenomenon in church history, or has it always been present to some degree? And is the legitimate, biblical gift of tongues only and exclusively the supernatural ability to speak a known language, so that speaking in an "unknown tongue" is by definition mere "gibberish" and illegitimate? Bitter battles have been fought over these issues.

While these are important questions historically, they are not central to the argument of this book. Volumes have been written as to whether tongues-speaking is eccentric or normal in church history, and the matter still isn't resolved. When tongues and other charismatic gifts do attract attention, this is often in the early period of a wave of renewal. Accurate historical assessment of renewal movements is notoriously difficult. Such movements are often considered heretical or at least eccentric, with the result that their literature is usually suppressed, and we have to evaluate them through the writings of their opponents. (This may be one of the best arguments for the divine inspiration of the New Testament; would such writings otherwise have survived?) Thus tongues-speaking may have been, in the words of John Nichol, "not a religious innovation," but a phenomenon that "in one form or another . . . has manifested itself throughout the history of the Christian Church."[1] But this is not the real issue.

The key issue is what a person *concludes* from the frequency or infrequency of glossolalia in history. For those opposed to tongues-speaking, the syllogism runs as follows: If tongues-speaking were a normative gift of the Spirit, it would always be present in the church; it has not always been present in the church; therefore it is not a normative gift of the Spirit. We would take issue with the major premise here, however, regardless of the historical question. The frequency or infrequency of tongues-speaking in church history says nothing, *necessarily*, about its legitimacy. Many things that *should* be normative in the life of the church have in fact not been.

One of the arguments against the doctrine of regeneration or justification by faith was, in some periods and contexts, that it was an innovation. Yet few today would argue that preaching the New Birth is illegitimate because it hasn't always been preached. We would agree here with John Wesley: The charismatic gifts largely disappeared, not because they were illegitimate, but because of spiritual decline in the church (see more on this in chapter 4, "The Charismatic Wesley"). Our view is that tongues-speaking is legitimate whenever it is prompted by the Holy Spirit, regardless of one's theology!

We would argue similarly with regard to the language/non-language question. In most cases the evidence is not sufficient to determine conclusively whether demonstrations of the Spirit did or did not include glossolalia, and whether possible instances of glossolalia involved known languages or non-language ecstatic utterance. As we will make clear in chapter 6, however, these distinctions may not be as significant as they seem. In the following analysis we do not attempt to distinguish between these kinds of tongues-speaking except where the evidence seems clear and unambiguous. Our reason for this is that often the language/non-language distinction is inserted into the discussion illegitimately, for polemical reasons. We want to leave the question open to avoid the danger of premature judgments.

THE FIRST THREE CENTURIES

The first Christians "continued to meet together in the temple courts. They broke bread in their homes and ate together with glad and sincere hearts, praising God . . ." (Acts 2:46–47). The pattern was spontaneity within a basic order which was probably based initially on Jewish synagogue tradition. The Corinthian church apparently went overboard on the side of spontaneity, with an overemphasis on speaking in tongues. First Corinthians 14 is Paul's plea to that church to practice the spontaneous and prophetic elements of worship within the bounds of order and spiritual common sense, without denying either.

Evelyn Underhill rightly notes that, from the first, Christian worship has been

> both liturgic and prophetic, historical and mystical, sacramental and spontaneous. . . . In Catholicism, the liturgic and sacramental element has decisively triumphed. The Evangelical Churches have restored, perhaps sometimes to excess, the prophetic and Biblical strand; whilst in those frequent revivals of free worship and claims to a direct experience of the Spirit which shock the decorum of the traditionalist, we see the continued power of the charismatic strain. But a full and balanced Christian cultus would find room for all these elements, and means of harmonizing and controlling them. . . .[2]

Maintaining this balance is a constant challenge. A biblical balance provides a channel through which the Spirit can work mightily. But what constitutes a balanced worship experience? Frankly, we know relatively little about early Christian worship patterns or about the degree of variety from one community to another.

The New Testament, however, shows two basic kinds of meetings: larger assemblies, and smaller, probably more informal home gatherings. Both presumably made room for varieties of worship gifts, if 1 Corinthians

14 is at all representative. It seems likely that in the first century at least, the larger assemblies were comparatively more liturgical and more indebted to synagogue patterns, while the home meetings were more informal and spontaneous and perhaps more varied. But it is impossible to be dogmatic about this.

Threats of heresy and schism during the period following the Apostolic Age set the church on a course toward institutionalization. The church through early councils agreed on the canon of Scripture and developed its creeds. It gradually became more liturgical and institutional. While theological definition was necessary in the light of attack, controversy, and divisions, one negative consequence of these institutionalizing tendencies was that teaching on the Holy Spirit and spiritual gifts was largely neglected. Glossolalia declined or was suppressed. Morton Kelsey suggests,

> Since most people were already irrational enough about Christianity, describing glossolalia would have been to magnify this sign into wild rumor. These first writers had had a good dose of the hatred that came from such rumors, accusations that Christians ate newborn babies, or conjured up crop failures and floods and earthquakes. They were trying to be rational in the face of so much feeling. . . . Talking about tongues would only have added fuel to the fire that flamed into irrational rejection of Christians as monsters, or, at best, queer people.[3]

In any case, with time the prophetic and spontaneous elements of worship were largely replaced by decorum, liturgy, and ritual. This trend was not endorsed by all thinking Christians of the time, however. Origen, for instance (about A.D. 185–254), though he discredited accounts of speaking in tongues and rejected its validity, was perhaps the most noteworthy charismatic (gift of grace) advocate of the third century. Origen believed that it was not ordination but having and practicing the *charismata* that supplied the necessary qualifications for teachers, pastors, and other leaders. He objected to the growing notion that presbyters and bishops were successors to the apostles. Instead he demanded that people in positions of leadership be characterized by charismatic authority.[4] As a model Origen proposed Moses' selection of Joshua as his successor:

> Here is no popular acclamation, no thought given to consanguinity or kinship; . . . the government of the people is handed over to him whom God has chosen, to a man who . . . has in him the Spirit of God and keeps the precepts of God in high sight. Moses knew from personal experience that he was preeminent in the law and in knowledge, so that the children of Israel should obey him.[5]

Origen maintained that the church had fallen into a sorry state, not because God failed in raising up leaders endowed with *charismata*, but because the church often did not recognize these people or give them proper honor and responsibility. The result was a dual hierarchy in the church, one consisting of the official hierarchy, the other of spiritually mature and gifted but obscure leaders. Origen goes so far as to assert in his commentary on Matthew 16:13–20 that those who recognize Jesus as the Christ as Peter did can become what Peter was. Thus the words of Jesus to Peter apply to other believers as well: "You are Peter, and on this rock I will build my church, and the gates of Hades will not overcome it" (v. 18).

Origen's criteria for true successors to Peter were charismatic: spiritual insight and holiness of life, not official position. He also felt that intellectual abilities acquired through disciplined study qualified as gifts of grace. Thus he represented what many today consider a contradiction in terms—the charismatic intellectual.[6]

Origen had a clear vision of how the church should function. However, the charismatic leadership he envisioned was not to be. In spite of Origen's objections, the church had already acquired an institutional structure that tended to repress charismatic leadership and the spontaneous use of grace gifts. This trend continued as the Catholic Church established itself as the universal manifestation of Christ on earth.

The earliest known description of the church as "catholic" (universal) appears in Ignatius' letter to the church in Smyrna in which he declares, "wherever Jesus Christ is, there is the Catholic Church."[7] By the end of the second century the church as "catholic" signified both orthodoxy (right belief) and universality. Latourette identifies three motives in this development of the Catholic Church: "to unite all Christians in conscious fellowship . . . , to preserve, transmit, and spread the Christian Gospel in its purity . . . , [and] to bring all Christians together into a visible 'body of Christ.' "[8]

The "catholic" designation also served to distinguish beliefs considered to be orthodox from those of professed Christians thought to be deviating from true Christianity. Increasingly regular gatherings, or synods, of bishops were called to root out heresy and to establish creeds. The first synod of record was held in Asia Minor to deal with Montanism, which was condemned as heretical.[9] Most noteworthy of the early synods was the first Council of Nicea in A.D. 325, at which the newly converted Emperor Constantine was a key figure. The Nicene Creed, or Confession, was adopted at this meeting, and Arianism was condemned.

After the first century, only a few references to tongues-speaking are found in Christian history until the modern period. This has led many Christians to conclude that the charismatic gifts in general, and the gift of tongues in particular, disappeared from the church after the apostolic era, never to reappear. This, however, is a faulty conclusion. Pro-charismatic writings in the early church were often destroyed by those who questioned their orthodoxy. Yet some literature does exist that suggests intermittent outbreaks of tongues-speaking and other charismatic phenomena.[10]

A few cryptic "sayings" attributed to Montanus and his disciples Priscilla and Maximilla suggest that a movement of the second century in Phrygia prophesied and spoke in tongues. It called itself "The New Prophecy" at the time and later came to be called Montanism. Because the movement taught that these gifts were reserved to themselves alone, the survival of Montanism until the fifth century offers no proof that the *charismata* continued in the church generally.[11] Unfortunately, most of our information about the Montanists derives from Eusebius and subsequent mainline historians opposed to the movement.[12]

Tertullian, a prominent church father of the early third century, became a Montanist in later life and was critical of the majority church until his death. Some historians maintain that Tertullian was quite specific about the existence and value of glossolalia. Others point out the influence of Montanism on Tertullian's writings and contend that the references are ambiguous. In the fourth century Chrysostom, like Origen earlier, discredited accounts of speaking in tongues and rejected its validity. Apparently the phenomenon was still in evidence, or the debate would not have surfaced.[13]

Speaking in tongues may still have been practiced in the fifth century, for Augustine makes reference to it. Augustine's argument is that tongues-speaking in the New Testament sense has become superfluous because the church is now universal:

> Why is it that no man speaks in the tongues of all nations? Because the Church itself now speaks in the tongues of all nations. Before, the Church was in one nation, where it spoke in the tongues of all. By speaking then in the tongues of all, it signified what was to come to pass; that by growing

among the nations, it would speak in the tongues of all. . . .
The Church, spread among the nations, speaks in all
tongues; the Church is the body of Christ, in this body thou
art a member: therefore, since thou art a member of that
body which speaks with all tongues, believe that thou too
speakest with all tongues.[14]

Vinson Synan observes that with time "the cessation
of the charismata became part of the classical theology of
the church. Augustine and Chrysostom were quoted by
countless theologians and commentators in the centuries
that followed."[15] This viewpoint, combined with the
reaction against Montanism and other early occurrences
of the *charismata*, prevailed in the church until modern
times.

Montanism and other manifestations of glossolalia
appear to have had virtually no influence on the creeds or
the establishment of the Roman Catholic episcopate,
except as their existence may have prompted the church
to institutionalize more quickly than it might have done
otherwise. Indeed, the Nicene Creed promulgated in A.D.
325 makes no mention whatsoever of the Holy Spirit.[16] At
the Second Ecumenical Council in A.D. 381, numerous
additions to the Nicene Creed were introduced, including
the phrase, "I believe in the Holy Ghost, the Lord, the
Giver of Life, who proceedeth from the Father, who with
the Father and the Son together is worshipped and
glorified, who spake by the prophets."[17] But this reference was prompted by the theological question of the
relation of the Spirit to the Father and Son, not by issues
relating to the *charismata*.

TONGUES IN THE EASTERN CHURCH

Both the Protestant and Catholic branches of the
American church derive from the Latin or Roman Catholic
tradition of the West. With the fall of the Roman Empire
and the disintegration of government due to barbarian

invasions, the church survived as the major institution of civilized life. Out of necessity it assumed many functions of secular government. It became authoritative and practical, stressing tradition and order rather than individual experience.

Another Christian tradition, the Greek Orthodox Church in the East, experienced very different cultural conditions at Constantinople than the Western church experienced in Rome. Partly for this reason the Greek church has maintained a rather different attitude toward the *charismata*. Kelsey notes,

> At Constantinople a strong central government provided the base for a brilliant and colorful civilization which never passed through the throes of the Dark Ages. Indeed its capital city remained secure against pagan invasion until 1451. Thus the church was never forced to take over the secular functions which were forced upon the Western church. The Greek church remained far more otherworldly and mystical. It continued the Greek bent of introspection and individuality. Greek monasticism, even though it came to play an important part in Byzantine politics, was never as organized or controlled as that which grew up in the West. There was a strain of wild enthusiasm and individualism in the Greek way which could make a saint of a man who sat for years on a solitary pillar. The East developed a mystical, individualistic, otherworldly, introverted Christianity. In this tradition the individual gifts of the Spirit flourished. The door was never closed to experiences like tongues.[18]

As an example of how the *charismata* functioned in the Greek church, Kelsey notes that the "One Hundred and Two Canons" established by the sixth council of the Eastern church in A.D. 691 contains a law forbidding laymen to teach unless they have the grace-gift of teaching. This emphasis on the *charismata* suggests that authority to teach comes from God, based on a gift of grace, and not simply from ecclesiastical authority. The same would be true of the other grace-gifts. Kelsey concludes, "While historical evidence of tongues within the Greek tradition has not been compiled, it is a fair inference that tongue speaking, being no more bizarre than other Eastern monastic practices, has simply continued within the tradition of Greek monasticism without attracting much notice."[19] Similarly, E. Glenn Hinson suggests that Orthodox monasticism considers tongues-speaking and other *charismata* "traditional and not uncommon, extending back through the centuries, perhaps even through the Middle Ages."[20]

PRE-REFORMATION

In contrast to the Greek church, the medieval church centered in Rome often seemed intent on weeding out all charismatic tendencies. Yet a number of popular religious movements sprang up that stressed the use of grace-gifts, whether or not they practiced tongues-speaking. Often gifts were recognized and practiced independently of the established ecclesiastical order in groups that were seeking to recapture New Testament Christianity.

An example would be the Waldensians, a kind of medieval "charismatic renewal." Peter Waldo was a rich merchant of Lyons, France. In 1176 he chose to distribute his wealth among the poor and beg for his own daily bread. Taking no purse, he preached in city and country as Christ had commanded his apostles. Others imitated Waldo, calling themselves the "Poor Men of Lyons." Although the Pope excommunicated them in 1184, the movement spread rapidly to Spain, Italy, Germany, and Bohemia. Noted for their simple dress, industrious labor, chastity, temperance, truthful speech, and belief that accumulating wealth was evil, these "heretics" were persecuted by the church and civil authorities. Those who survived settled primarily in the valleys of the Italian Alps. The established church would encounter their views again at the time of the Reformation.[21]

The Lollards, a group of John Wycliffe's followers in England, may be another example. Likewise, several groups of followers of John Hus, including the Hussites, Utraquists, and Taborites, were in many ways charismatic. They recognized various gifts and often provided wide opportunity for "lay" ministry. Equally significant, these groups provided spiritual ancestors and precedents to the Protestant Reformation. They prepared the way for an increased outpouring of the Holy Spirit and his gifts in the church.

The church of the Middle Ages was not, of course, entirely devoid of Spirit-led leaders nor was it intent on stamping out all charismatic manifestations. Monasticism provided some space for the *charismata;* mysticism, in which gifts of grace were sometimes in evidence, flourished throughout this period.[22] But the long sweep of history suggests that if charismatic phenomena and ministry were few and far between, this was due in no small part either to repression or to a general lack of spiritual vitality in the institutional church.[23]

THE REFORMATION: SPIRITUAL PRIESTHOOD AND SPIRITUAL GIFTS

The Protestant Reformation of the sixteenth century was the most organized and popular dissenting force to shake the Catholic Church. It was soon powerful enough that the church could not suppress it. The religious controversies of the Reformation focused primarily on other areas of theology, so that little attention was given to the gifts of the Spirit. The focus was on rooting out corruption in the church and restoring the primacy of salvation by faith as grounded in Scripture, not on the restoration of the *charismata.*

Kenneth Kinghorn writes, "The Lutheran and Reformed theologians seldom mentioned spiritual gifts. . . .

When Luther discussed spiritual gifts he identified them with talents or material blessings."[24] It is worth noting, however, that one of Luther's most radical doctrines—the priesthood of believers—relates directly to spiritual gifts. Luther himself made this connection, as his writings show.

The link between the priesthood of believers and the gifts of the Spirit in Luther's thought has received relatively little attention. That is probably because Luther did not stress the gifts of the Spirit as much as other aspects of the universal priesthood. Yet, without this emphasis Luther's doctrine of the priesthood of believers appears more static than he himself apparently conceived it to be.

Commenting on 1 Peter 4:10–11, which mentions the *charismata*, Luther notes, ". . . we should serve one another. With what? With the gifts of God which everyone has received. The Gospel wants everyone to be the other person's servant and, in addition, to see that he remains in the gift which he has received, that is, in the position to which he has been called."[25]

Luther goes on to say, "God has poured out varied gifts among the people. They should be directed to only one end, namely, that one person should serve the other person with them, especially those who are in authority, whether with preaching or with another office."[26]

Elsewhere Luther refers to the Pauline passages on spiritual gifts in speaking of the priesthood of believers. In his sermon on Psalm 110:4 he observes,

> Out of the multitude of Christians some must be selected who shall lead the others by virtue of the special gifts and aptitude which God gives them for the office. Thus St. Paul writes (Eph. 4:11, 12): "And His gifts were that some should be apostles, some prophets, some evangelists, some pastors and teachers, for the equipment of the saints . . . , for the work of the ministry, for the building up of the body of Christ. . . ."[27]

In his sermon on Psalm 110:3 Luther specifically relates the priesthood of all believers to the gifts of the Spirit:

> Here the prophet applies the priestly office and adornment to the Christians, the people of the New Testament. He says that their worship of God is to consist in the beautiful and glorious priesthood of those who are always in the presence of God and perform nothing but holy sacrifices. . . .
>
> Well, what is this "holy adornment," these priestly garments which adorn the Christians so that they become His holy priesthood? Nothing else than the beautiful, divine, and various gifts of the Holy Spirit, as St. Paul (Eph. 4:11, 12) and St. Peter (1 Peter 4:10) say, which were given to Christendom to advance the knowledge and the praise of God. . . .
>
> Their adornment is different from the external splendor, the gold, precious jewels, and silks of the Levitical priests. . . . The chrism, anointing, and priestly ordination He bestows is quite different; it is the Holy Spirit who adorns them in glory and holiness and clothes them in His power and with His gifts.[28]

Luther does not seem to have worked out exactly how the Christian community identifies the varying spiritual gifts, although he seems to see these gifts related to offices and to some degree synonymous with vocations.[29] Presumably he would feel that the church, led by the Spirit and the Word, would be directed to select as public ministers those who had received the appropriate spiritual gifts. Significantly, Luther did see the exercise of priestly functions within the Christian community as animated by the vivifying presence and ministry of the Holy Spirit through the gifts. But Luther never carried either the priesthood of believers or the gifts of the Spirit to their logical and practical conclusion for normal church life.

John Calvin's teachings on the Holy Spirit shed little light for us, since Calvin maintained that supernatural gifts of the Spirit ceased with the apostles.[30] When Calvin spoke of gifts, he tended to identify them with offices of leadership in the church. Thus, he says, in commenting on Ephesians 4:11,

> Now, we might be surprised that, when he is speaking of the gifts of the Holy Spirit, Paul should enumerate offices instead of gifts. I reply, whenever men are called by God, gifts are connected with offices. For God does not cover men with a mask in appointing them apostles or pastors, but also furnishes them with gifts, without which they cannot properly discharge their office.[31]

Calvin adds, "That we have ministers of the Gospel is His gift; that they excel in necessary gifts is His gift; that they execute the trust committed to them is likewise His gift."[32]

It is understandable then, surveying the historical landscape, that Kinghorn concludes, "Whatever contributions early theologians have made—and they have been many—a theology of spiritual gifts has not been one of them. The subject is seldom touched on in the writings of most of the Christian leaders of the past."[33]

Yet there is some irony in these theologians' failure to embrace a fully charismatic posture. Vinson Synan observes,

> One of the charges leveled against the Reformers by the Catholic authorities was that Protestantism lacked authenticating miracles confirming their beginnings. To Catholic theologians, charismata were seen as divine approval at the beginning of the church. Catholics demanded of Luther and Calvin signs and wonders to attest to their authenticity as true, orthodox Christian churches.[34]

While the Reformation was not characterized by glossolalia, or even by an emphasis on *charismata* in general, yet it was a significant movement of the Spirit and paved the way for a tolerance of varieties of religious expression. This is especially evident among the "Radical Reformers" of the Anabaptist branch of the Reformation.

Historian Richard Quebedeaux asserts that tongues-speaking was occasionally practiced among them.[35]

Both the Reformed and Anabaptist streams of the Reformation, therefore, in their own ways helped to set the stage for Methodism and subsequently the Holiness Movement, which in turn provided fertile soil for the modern manifestation of the *charismata* in the Pentecostal and Charismatic movements.

GLOSSOLALIA SINCE THE REFORMATION

Instances of glossolalia and other grace-gifts increased after the Reformation both on the Continent and in England. Quebedeaux notes, "Various splinter groups of the early Quakers espoused speaking in tongues as a significant religious experience—among these, the so-called Ranters in England."[36] The Ranters flourished briefly during the English Commonwealth in the mid-seventeenth century, but the movement was rejected by other Quakers.

Another group manifesting the *charismata* were the Jansenists, a reform movement in the Roman Catholic church that flourished in France in the seventeenth and early eighteenth centuries. In revoking the Edict of Nantes, Quebedeaux writes,

> Louis XIV of France called upon the Protestant Huguenots to return to the Roman Catholic Church, and reinforced his urgings with severe persecution. During this time, some of the Huguenots (the Camisards) reported phenomena among them such as "strange sounds in the air; the sound of a trumpet and a harmony of voices." Those affected were known as "prophets of the Cevennes mountains," and the episodes continued until 1711.[37]

Some members of this group fled to England amid persecution and were called the "French Prophets." They are believed to have influenced Mother Ann Lee and the Wardleys, originators of the Shakers, to adopt the practice of speaking in tongues. The Shakers also practiced the gift of healing. In 1774 they carried their practices to America. Quebedeaux writes, "According to clergymen who examined her, Ann Lee, although only semiliterate, spoke in several known languages."[38]

John and Charles Wesley knew of the French Prophets and had contact with them on at least one occasion, as we will see in chapter 4.

Closer to the modern era, one of the best documented occurrences of glossolalia involved the Irvingites.

Edward Irving, who was born in 1792, the year after Wesley died, was pastor of a Presbyterian church on Regents Square in London in the 1830s. A popular preacher, he spoke often on the need for renewal of the apostolic gifts, especially those of healing and speaking in tongues. When a renewal actually began in October, 1831, it caused a minor sensation in the city. Thomas Carlyle even suggested in his *Reminiscences* that a bucket of water be dumped on the "hysterical madwoman," Mary Campbell, a former invalid who was suddenly healed and spoke in an unknown tongue while friends were praying for her. She lived out a healthy life and became a prominent spokesperson for the movement.

Irving never received the gift of tongues himself, but the phenomenon continued in his church for months. The eloquent preacher was the center of controversy for other teachings in addition to the *charismata*, and the Presbytery of London eventually convicted Irving of heresy. In the meantime, some of his followers organized the Catholic Apostolic Church, which taught that the *charismata* had been restored. Though the new church organization soon waned, the Irvingite experience contributed to the expectation of many Christians for a charismatic outpouring of the Holy Spirit.[39]

Other movements which, like the Irvingites, grew out of the Anglo-American revivalism of the 1830s and

1840s manifested the *charismata* to one degree or another. In the United States they included groups as diverse as Mormons and converts of Charles G. Finney's revival campaigns. All these groups documented pre-twentieth-century cases of tongues-speaking. It is probable that these occurrences are not isolated instances. Robert Anderson observes, "If we turn to individual instances of speaking in tongues . . . , it is quite possible that such have occurred sporadically throughout Christian history. . . ."[40]

But none of these events had wide-ranging and lasting influence on the church at large. The nineteenth century drew to a close with the church on the threshold of a charismatic resurgence greater than any she had experienced since the first century.

CONCLUSION

We have seen that manifestations of *charismata* in general, and of glossolalia in particular, have recurred periodically in church history. Yet, as Quebedeaux points out, ". . . it is only since this [20th] century began that the church as a whole has been confronted by a widespread manifestation of the Pentecostal experience within its ranks. . . . [see ch. 3] What is striking . . . is the relatively large amount of favor shown toward the Pentecostal movement as a whole (even toward glossolalia), which was not evident in most earlier studies."[41]

Before the Reformation most movements of a charismatic nature were branded as heretical and either died out or dwindled to small groups of minor significance. To a large extent this was due to the structure, power, and influence of the extensive Roman Catholic Church. Perhaps it was also due to poor organizational skills and leadership ability of charismatic leaders, though often key leaders were martyred in the early stages of renewal movements.

Even after the Reformation, charismatic movements tended to be offshoots from larger movements and lacked the staying power of the ecclesiastical forces that gave them birth.

In light of this, it is striking that charismatic renewal today has the blessing of the Pope, is led by educated and influential leaders, and is pervading both Catholic and Protestant circles. George Carey writes that "It is the only revival in history which has united evangelicals on the one hand, with their strong emphasis on the death of Christ and full atonement, and Roman Catholics on the other, with their emphasis on the sacraments. Somehow charismatic experiences have brought together people who on the face of it have little in common theologically."[42]

Clearly, charismatic renewal has become a major force in church history. We turn now to examine the shape of charismatic renewal today and the issues it raises.

STUDY QUESTIONS

1. Although the word "charismatic" is often used to describe a person who speaks in tongues, we have seen that it has a much broader biblical meaning. In the light of this broader meaning, what other practices or aspects of your church might be labeled "charismatic"?

2. Do some programs or activities in your church *not* seem to be based in the operation of God's grace? If so, do you think these programs or activities in any way restrict the way the Holy Spirit would like to function?

3. Pretend that Origen were alive today and could walk into your church to meet with believers. What comments might he make concerning the way your church

functions? How do you feel about his criticisms of the church of his own time? Were they valid? Are they relevant to your church today?

4. The Protestant Reformation brought about dramatic changes in the direction the church would take in the centuries that followed. Some modern church leaders think Charismatic renewal will ultimately affect the church as dramatically as the Reformation did. What do you think?

3

A NEW PENTECOST?

Since the early 1960s North American Christians have had to deal with new questions about the church. The Charismatic renewal, through informal contacts, extensive literature, and such popular television programs as "The 700 Club," has led increasing numbers of believers to see the church as in some sense charismatic. Just what this means may be unclear or widely disputed. Nevertheless, the Charismatic renewal has forced nearly all Christian traditions to reexamine what Scripture teaches about the *charismata*.

To set these questions in perspective, this chapter will trace the rise of the modern Charismatic renewal, going back to the emergence of Pentecostalism at the beginning of this century. Then we will ask, What is the *real* "charismatic question" facing the church today?

THE RISE OF PENTECOSTALISM

Many Holiness denominations arose in the heartland of America during the 1890s and after, principally as a result of the Holiness Movement of the 1860s and 1870s. The Church of the Nazarene, the Pilgrim Holiness Church, and dozens of other small and conservative

Wesleyan groups were born out of the ferment of Holiness revivals and associations and in reaction to the perceived doctrinal drift of Methodism. These groups stressed Wesley's "second work of grace" doctrine with its expectation of a second crisis experience of "entire sanctification."[1]

Holiness theology and practice, with a growing anticipation of mighty works of the Holy Spirit in these "latter days," provided fertile soil for the rise of Pentecostalism—a new movement that in its early stages was identified almost exclusively with the practice of tongues-speaking.

The Rev. Charles Fox Parham of Kansas is credited with being the first to formally state a doctrine of "glossolalia" as the only evidence of baptism with the Holy Spirit. He began teaching this view after an outbreak of tongues-speaking early on January 1, 1901, at Parham's Bible school near Topeka. Parham maintained that tongues should be a normal part of Christian worship, not an unusual phenomenon of religious enthusiasm. This teaching laid the initial foundation for the modern Pentecostal Movement.[2]

From 1901 to 1905 Parham conducted a whirlwind revival tour that spread his Pentecostal doctrine to key locations in Kansas and Missouri. In 1905 he moved his headquarters to Houston, Texas, and for a few months operated a Bible training school that enrolled about twenty-five students. One student, W. J. Seymour, received his theological training there at the time.[3]

A poor Southern Holiness preacher, Seymour accepted an invitation to pastor a Negro mission in Los Angeles that was associated with the Church of the Nazarene. In his first sermon among the Nazarenes, Seymour emphasized the importance of speaking in tongues. The next night Seymour found the church door padlocked, and he with no place to stay. A Richard

Asbury took him in, and nightly prayer and preaching services accompanied by unusual religious ecstasy were held in the Asbury living room. News of the unusual events spread through the neighborhood, and the rapidly growing crowd moved to the front porch and soon spilled into the street.

A search for larger quarters led Seymour to a decrepit, abandoned Methodist Church building at 312 Azusa Street most recently used as a tenement house and livery stable.[4] The revival services conducted there soon received national attention, much of it less than complimentary. "Breathing strange utterances and mouthing a creed which it would seem no sane mortal could understand, the newest sect has started," wrote a skeptical *Los Angeles Times* reporter on April 18, 1906. The front-page article further observed,

> . . . In a tumble-down shack on Azusa Street, . . . devotees practice fanatical rites, preach the wildest theories and work themselves into a state of mad excitement. . . . Colored people and a sprinkling of whites compose the congregation, and . . . the worshippers spend hours swaying forth and back in a nerve-racking attitude of prayer and supplication. They claim to have the "gift of tongues" and to be able to comprehend the babel.[5]

The Azusa Street revival continued for three years and is commonly regarded as the beginning of the modern Pentecostal Movement. It acted as a catalyst that congealed the practice of tongues-speaking into a fully defined doctrine. Almost every Pentecostal group in existence today can trace its lineage directly or indirectly back to Azusa Street. To give just one example, G. B. Cashwell of Dunn, North Carolina, briefly visited Azusa Street, then returned home, where he rented a former tobacco warehouse and began a similar series of meetings. Vinson Synan writes that Cashwell's Pentecostal meetings ". . . would be for the southeastern area of the

United States what the Azusa Street meeting had been to the western area . . . [resulting in] the conversion of most of the holiness movement in the Southeast to the pentecostal view."[6]

In all, some twenty-five separate denominations sprang from Pentecostalism within fourteen years. These became the most rapidly growing group of churches in North America during the first half of the twentieth century.

THE MODERN CHARISMATIC MOVEMENT

Whereas Pentecostalism experienced a violent birth among the poor who subscribed to Holiness theology, the current Charismatic renewal seems to have cropped up in many different churches at once, both Protestant and Catholic, conservative and liberal. A search for roots of the movement leads to such diverse people as Pentecostal minister David Du Plessis, Episcopal rector Dennis Bennett, students at Yale University, and evangelist Oral Roberts:

- In 1951 David du Plessis, former executive secretary of the Pentecostal Fellowship in South Africa, discovered to his amazement that leaders of the World Council of Churches extended a warm welcome when he felt led to visit their headquarters and witness to them. Since then, he has traveled extensively, providing a new understanding of Pentecostalism to a wide variety of Christians.[7]

- Meanwhile, at St. Mark's Episcopal Church in Van Nuys, California, Dennis Bennett saw his parish grow to two thousand from 1953 to 1961, fueled by small groups centered on Bible study and prayer. One group practiced a wide range of spiritual gifts, including prayer in tongues. When Bennett related to his congregation that the work of the Holy Spirit in his own life included praying in tongues, he was asked to resign. He did so, but invitations to speak elsewhere and his writings on the subject have encouraged Charismatic renewal in many small fellowship groups in a wide variety of mainline Protestant denominations.[8]

● In 1962 Charismatic renewal took hold among students who participated in the Inter-Varsity Christian Fellowship at Yale. The following year saw similar events take place at Penn State, Kent State in Ohio, Indiana University, Purdue, and elsewhere.[9]

● Beginning in the late 1950s the television ministry of Pentecostal Holiness evangelist Oral Roberts introduced millions of Americans to Pentecostalism. Students from Oral Roberts University, established in 1965 in Tulsa, Oklahoma, have broadened this influence. The scope of Roberts' impact was dramatically demonstrated in 1968 with the transferral of his ordination to the United Methodist Church. Bishop Angie Smith of Oklahoma made it clear to Roberts that no change in his views was expected and that the Methodist Church needed what Roberts preached.[10]

Many similar occurrences could be noted. They all show that the renewal is broad-based, cutting across denominational, ethnic, educational, and economic boundaries. Charles Hummel writes,

> . . . the renewal is not a movement. . . . It cannot be traced to one outstanding leader and his followers with the stamp of their doctrinal and organizational convictions. Nor is it like the modern ecumenical movement which was initiated by theological scholars and church leaders. Rather, the

Charismatic renewal started as a pattern of events in the lives of a wide variety of Christians. This pattern comes to focus in the exercise of the full range of spiritual gifts (charisms) for strengthening the body of Christ in worship, evangelism and service.[11]

One of the most significant forces behind the growth of Charismatic renewal has been the Full Gospel Business Men's Fellowship International (FGBMFI). Members of FGBMFI are linked by mutual business concerns as well as by a desire to use their influence and financial resources to effectively communicate their Christian faith. Established in the early 1950s by dairy farmer Demos Shakarian at the urging of Oral Roberts, the FGBMFI bridges the gap between Pentecostals and mainline Protestants, and Catholic author Kevin Ranaghan credits it with providing the greatest Protestant contribution to Charismatic renewal in the Catholic church.[12]

People associated with the modern Charismatic renewal are often lumped into the catch-all category of "Neo-Pentecostal." Tongues remains a dominant practice among them, but not to the exclusion of the other gifts and emphases. They have many theological differences, but exhibit a common interest in seeing the gospel advanced through practicing all the gifts of grace.

In recent years the Charismatic Movement has so infiltrated evangelical colleges and seminaries that by 1983, Pentecostals and charismatics accounted for about one-third of the students at Fuller and Gordon-Conwell seminaries, both of which are large, independent, and influential institutions.

"Signs, Wonders and Church Growth" became the most popular course ever offered at Fuller Theological Seminary. Taught by John Wimber and Peter Wagner, this course studied the use of the gifts of the Spirit in the churches. Classes often ended with tongues-speaking, prophesying, and prayer for the sick. Wimber's "Vineyard Christian Fellowship" congregation in Yorba Linda, California, put the classroom theories into practice. At that time some four thousand people were attending Sunday worship services in the Yorba Linda church that in 1982 was only five years old.[13] The so-called Vineyard Movement continues to grow, having an impact not only in California but across the continent and even beyond the U.S. Some observers now view this renewed emphasis on gifts, healing, and "power evangelism" as the cutting edge of charismatic renewal today.

THE CATHOLIC CHARISMATIC RENEWAL

In the early 1960s Pope John XXIII called for a council in Rome to "open the windows" and renew the church. Some twenty-five hundred leaders (including non-Catholic observers) from around the world gathered to investigate what could be done. This was Vatican II, a conclave lasting three years (1962 to 1965). The Pope set the stage when, in his address at the opening of the council he declared that "the substance of the ancient doctrine of the deposit of faith is one thing, and the way it is presented is another."[14] He asked every Catholic in the world to pray daily: "Lord, renew your wonders in this our day as by a new Pentecost."[15]

A key statement at Vatican II by Leon Joseph Cardinal Suenens of Belgium set the stage for approval of the Charismatic outbreak that occurred only three years later:

> To St. Paul, the Church of Christ does not appear as some administrative organization, but as a living, organic ensemble of gifts, charisms and services. The Holy Spirit is given to all Christians, and to each one in particular; and He in turn gives to each and every one gifts and charisms "which differ according to the grace bestowed upon us" (Rom. 12:6).[16]

Many striking changes shook the Catholic Church after the Second Vatican Council, but none was more significant than the Catholic Charismatic Renewal, which began in North America.[17] The movement was born at Duquesne University in Pittsburgh in 1966 when Ralph Kiefer and Bill Storey, two lay theology professors, read *The Cross and the Switchblade* by David Wilkerson and *They Speak With Other Tongues* by John Sherrill. With the help of an Episcopal priest at a Presbyterian prayer group, Kiefer and Storey "received the baptism" and spoke languages they had not learned. Soon afterward, on February 17–19, 1967, they held a weekend retreat in Pittsburgh, the first Catholic Pentecostal prayer meeting on record.

Retreat participants were asked to read *The Cross and the Switchblade* before the meeting. The retreat consisted of intensive study of the Book of Acts followed by a day of prayer and study. After a birthday party Saturday night for one of the priests, the entire group spontaneously gathered in the chapel for prayer. Some began speaking in tongues, others prophesied or received gifts of discernment or wisdom, and the group was united in a spirit of love.[18]

From Duquesne University the new movement spread to Notre Dame University in South Bend, Indiana, where acceptance among respected scholars and theologians gave credence and provided leadership. From Notre Dame, Catholic Charismatic Renewal caught fire throughout the United States and around the world.[19] Within six years the movement, comprising chiefly laypeople rather than clergy, claimed fifty thousand adherents.[20] Synan gives a dramatic summary:

> The burgeoning crowds that attended the various Catholic charismatic conferences during the 1970s sent many churchmen back to the theological drawing boards to make new assessments of the situation.

What became clear during that decade was that mainline charismatics had developed a new view of the "baptism in the Holy Spirit," which allowed Pentecostalism to flourish in the historic churches without the "cultural baggage" and rigid exclusivism espoused by the Pentecostal churches. The Wesleyan teaching of an instantaneous second experience of sanctification was not adopted by any of the new charismatic groups, although much stress was laid on holiness as the goal of the Spirit-filled Christian lifestyle.[21]

A WORLDWIDE MOVEMENT

Since the sixties, Charismatic renewal has become a worldwide movement. Synan writes, "One of the favorite aphorisms of the pentecostal pioneers went like this: 'In the early days, the critics said that the pentecostal movement would blow over in a few years—and it did, it blew over the whole world.' "[22]

The most rapid church growth in the world today that has been documented is taking place in South Korea, where the *charismata* are everywhere evident (though rapid growth has marked much of the Korean church for decades). Churches there are now growing on average at an annual rate of 6.6 percent, two-thirds of it by conversions. It is estimated that the population of South Korea will be 42 percent Christian by the end of the century if this trend continues.[23] Although we don't have statistics to prove it, the current Christian growth rate may be even higher in Central Africa. Rapid growth is also taking place in China, where it is estimated that the Christian population grew from 3 million in 1949 to 30 million in 1980.[24] Some China researchers put the total today at 50 million or more. Much though certainly not all of this growth is pentecostal in spirit.

Some church growth analysts go as far as to predict that more than one-half of the populations of Brazil and Chile will be Pentecostal by the end of the twentieth century.[25] Even if these predictions prove inaccurate, the fact remains that Pentecostal groups now comprise the largest family of Protestants in the world—more than 51 million. This is remarkable, given that before 1900 there was not even one Pentecostal church in the world.[26] Add to this the vast numbers of Charismatics who remain in the Catholic, Anglican, and mainline Protestant churches, and one must agree with Synan's observation that these groups and individuals "constitute the most vital and fastest-growing movement in the church since the days of the Reformation."[27]

Lumping together the various Pentecostal and Charismatic groups is not to ignore, of course, the considerable theological and sociological differences between these two major movements and (equally important) within them. Not all Pentecostals agree on points of Christology, soteriology, or even in their doctrine of the Holy Spirit. Some Pentecostal groups, such as the Assemblies of God, are more Calvinist in their basic orientation, while many tend to be more Wesleyan. As one would expect, wide theological differences separate Pentecostals with fundamentalist roots and the newer Charismatics who may be found in Presbyterian, Methodist, Lutheran, Roman Catholic, or Episcopal churches.

What all these groups do share, however, is (1) an emphasis on a personal experience of the Holy Spirit in one's life, and (2) the practice of the gift of tongues. Differences include such issues as whether tongues-speaking should be normative for all Christians; whether it is a necessary sign of being filled with the Spirit; the proper role and use of tongues-speaking in worship or as a "prayer language"; and the relationship between tongues-speaking and a range of discipleship and lifestyle issues. Behind these issues are often deeper issues of soteriology (the nature of salvation), ecclesiology (the meaning and shape of the church), and the nature of the Trinity (the relationship of Father, Son, and Holy Spirit).

The sociological differences between these various groups are equally intriguing. In *The New Charismatics*, Richard Quebedeaux discusses a number of differences between classical Pentecostalism and modern Charismatic Renewal, including differences in worship, ecclesiastical stance, and views toward culture. He notes that the sect/church typology of Ernst Troeltsch and H. Richard Niebuhr has at times been used here:

> Classical Pentecostalism has usually been regarded as illustrative of the sect-type religious organization in sociological typologies; while Charismatic Renewal, . . . because it is a movement largely *within* the historic Protestant, Anglican, and Eastern Orthodox denominations and the Roman Catholic Church, should be identified with the church- or denomination-type religious organization. Indeed, specific differences between Classical Pentecostalism and Neo-Pentecostalism (to a degree, at least) are reminiscent of the general variance between sect and denomination or church as ideal types.[28]

THE REAL CHARISMATIC QUESTION

While Charismatic currents in the church raise a number of issues, we believe the fundamental question is not the legitimacy of particular gifts but the more basic one of whether our churches are really charismatic in the biblical sense. Are we nurturing churches that function not merely on the basis of tradition and ecclesiastical structures, but also on the basis of the Spirit's work in the church both individually and corporately?

For both biblical and pragmatic reasons, the church needs all the gifts that the Spirit sovereignly chooses to give. James Dunn has written, "The inspiration, the concrete manifestations of Spirit in power, in revelation, in word, in service, all are necessary—for without them grace soon becomes status, gift becomes office, ministry becomes bureaucracy, body of Christ becomes institution, and *koinonia* becomes the extension fund."[29]

If our concern is with the vitality of our churches, Christians on all sides of this issue should approach "the Charismatic question" broadly and biblically, rather than narrowly and apologetically with reference to only certain gifts. As we noted in chapter 1, biblically we must affirm that the church is fundamentally charismatic.

As the very terms "Charismatic" and "Holiness" suggest, the issue between conservative Wesleyans on the one hand and Pentecostals and Charismatics on the other concerns two different points of emphasis: the church as holy or the church as charismatic. Wesleyans have stressed that Christians are to be holy; Pentecostals have emphasized the charismatic gifts. Sometimes this has come down to the question of the gifts versus the fruit of the Spirit. Yet in Scripture these two aspects of Christian experience are complementary, not in conflict. Without doubt, the church is to be holy, and Christians are to pursue that "holiness without which none will see the Lord" (Heb. 12:14 RSV). But the charismatic dimension of the church is fully as biblical as the stress on holiness.

The same Holy Spirit who sanctifies is the Spirit who gives gifts. The same Jesus Christ who apportions grace-gifts in the church is the Lord who has become our sanctification (1 Cor. 12:4–6). A biblical church will be *both* holy and charismatic, and all earnest Christians should be concerned that both the holiness and charismatic emphases are fully biblical.

We must see that these two emphases *really are* complementary. Each needs the other. The church needs both the cleansing, sanctifying work of the Spirit and His gracious bestowal of the variety of spiritual gifts taught in Scripture. The New Testament generally puts the charismatic emphasis in the context, in fact, of the call for Christians to be God's holy, love-filled people. The teaching about gifts in Romans 12:4–8 is preceded by a call to holiness and is followed by an emphasis on love.

Ephesians 4:11–16 shows us how the holy, charismatic Christian community is to function. On the one hand, a variety of equipping *charismata* is given "to prepare God's people for works of service" so that the body "grows and builds itself up in love, as each part does its work." On the other hand, believers are to attain "the fullnesses of perfection found in Christ." "Speaking the truth in love," they are "in all things" to "grow up into him who is the Head, that is, Christ." The two go together.

Kenneth Kinghorn stresses this in his balanced book, *Gifts of the Spirit*. "Without *love* spiritual gifts cater to human pride, and they become perverted. Without *gifts* love lacks the proper tools with which to function. When love and gifts combine, each gives meaning to the other," Kinghorn writes. So gifts, combined with love, have a crucial role in God's plan: "The church cannot function as God intends if Christians rely entirely on their human talents. Only through the *charismata* can Christ's disciples receive the divine enabling they need for their ministry."[30]

Theologians from varying perspectives have in recent years come to affirm the significance of charismatic gifts for the ministry of the whole body of believers. Jürgen Moltmann writes, "The whole congregation has 'spiritual' and charismatic gifts, not merely its 'spiritual' pastors. The whole congregation and every individual in it belongs with all their powers and potentialities to the mission of God's kingdom."[31]

One of the finest statements on the *charismata* comes from Catholic theologian Hans Küng. In an essay entitled "The Charismatic Structure of the Church" Küng argues that "to discover the charismata is to rediscover the real ecclesiology of St. Paul."[32] He rightly suggests that we misunderstand the *charismata* when we think of them "mainly as extraordinary, miraculous and sensational phenomena," when we limit them to only one kind or category, or when we deny their universal distribution to all believers.[33] "Thus every spiritual gift of whatever kind, every call is a charisma," he says, and "this infinite variety of the charismata implies their unlimited distribution in the Church."[34]

Küng adds, "All this implies . . . that [the *charismata*] are not a thing of the past (possible and real only in the early Church), but eminently contemporary and actual; they do not hover on the periphery of the Church but are eminently central and essential to it. In this sense one should speak of a *charismatic structure of the Church* which embraces and goes beyond the structure of its government."[35]

As these authors indicate, this emphasis becomes intensely practical for the life and ministry of the Christian community. "Where a Church or a community thrives only on officeholders and not on all the members," notes Küng, "one may well wonder in all seriousness whether the Spirit has not been thrown out with the charismata."[36]

The New Testament pictures believers individually and corporately growing up into the fullness of Christ through the exercise of gifts and progress in sanctification. The charismatic theme underscores something that we in the Holiness Movement have not emphasized enough: The "fullness of Christ"—which is our goal—refers not primarily to individual experience but to the corporate life of the believing community and to the fullness of grace in Jesus from which spiritual gifts flow. Sanctification, like the *charismata*, is for the Body of Christ and for each person in the Body. Sanctification is relational horizontally as well as vertically so that, as Wesley pointed out, we should see holiness as social, not solitary. This is, in fact, what Wesley meant when he said, "Christianity is essentially a social religion, and . . . to turn it into a solitary religion is indeed to destroy it."[37]

It is well for us to enquire how such an understanding of spiritual gifts squares with John Wesley's theology. Were his doctrine and practice of the church charismatic in the New Testament sense? To this question we now turn.

STUDY QUESTIONS

1. The Bible portrays no conflict between the gifts and the fruit of the Spirit. They function side by side, complementing one another. The church and individual Christians who make up the church should be both charismatic and holy. When conflict arises between these two essential aspects, what might be the source of that conflict?

2. Matthew 16:18 reads, "You are *Petros* (a rock), and on this rock I will build my church, and the powers of death shall not prevail against it." Why should the gates of hell shudder before a church that is both holy and charismatic?

3. What consequences do you see resulting from conflicts between the Charismatic and Holiness churches?

4. In what sense is it accurate to say that a biblically faithful church will be a charismatic church?

4

THE CHARISMATIC WESLEY

To be Wesleyan certainly requires us to examine John Wesley's theology. What were Wesley's own views regarding the *charismata*? Is Wesleyan Christianity a charismatic movement in the proper biblical sense? We will answer these questions first by looking at the theology of John Wesley himself, and then by noting parallels between the eighteenth-century Wesleyan Revival in England and contemporary Charismatic renewal.

WESLEY'S THEOLOGY

If we examine John Wesley's theology in the light of biblical charismatic themes, we discover that Wesley was charismatic. Yet this must be said with some qualifications. Wesley did not speak in tongues, so far as we know,[1] and in fact did not have to face this issue in the way we do today. Though he said comparatively little about the *charismata*, he did say more than most of his contemporaries. And if we view Christianity as charismatic in the proper biblical sense, we can quickly see that Wesley's theology is charismatic in the four ways that define the term as suggested in chapter 1.

1. *Wesley's theology is charismatic in its stress on God's grace in the life and experience of the church.* Wesley was deeply conscious of the operation of the grace of God in personal experience and in the life of the church—God's grace "preventing [or coming before], accompanying, and following" every person.[2]

Wesley was as deeply conscious of God's grace as were the leaders of the sixteenth-century Reformation. He had a deep optimism of grace that formed the foundation of his emphasis on the universal atonement, the witness of the Spirit, and Christian perfection. Wesley's stress on "preventing," or prevenient, grace is especially important and sets him apart from the earlier Reformers. Colin Williams has observed that Wesley "broke the chain of logical necessity by which the Calvinist doctrine of predestination seems to flow from the doctrine of original sin, by his doctrine of prevenient grace."[3]

This doctrine teaches that God's grace has been shed abroad indiscriminately to all people as an unconditional benefit of the Atonement, enabling them to take the initial steps toward God. Wesley argued, "There is no man that is in a state of mere nature; there is no man, unless he has quenched the Spirit, that is wholly void of the grace of God. No man living is entirely destitute of what is vulgarly called *natural conscience.* But this is not natural: It is more properly termed *preventing grace.* . . . no man sins because he has no grace, but because he does not use the grace which he hath."[4]

Wesley saw the whole plan of salvation as grounded in the grace of God. It follows that the church exists and lives by God's grace. Although Wesley said little specifically about the church being dependent on grace, this is the clear implication of his view. Whenever he discusses the church he stresses the spiritual, living meaning of it. Perhaps Wesley's most compact definition of the New Testament church is his comment on Acts 5:11: "A company of men, called by the gospel, grafted into Christ by baptism, animated by love, united by all kind of fellowship, and disciplined by the death of Ananias and Sapphira."[5] Wesley wrote in "A Letter to a Roman Catholic" in 1749,

> I believe that Christ by his Apostles gathered unto himself a Church, to which he has continually added such as shall be saved; that this catholic, that is, universal, Church, extending to all nations and all ages, is holy in all its members, who have fellowship with the holy angels, who constantly minister to these heirs of salvation; and with all the living members of Christ on earth, as well as all who are departed in his faith and fear.[6]

Wesley's view of the church was comprehensive and perhaps more charismatic than he knew, for he was charitable toward improper practices and even wrong doctrines if a congregation gave evidence of the Spirit's presence:

> Whoever they are that have "one Spirit, one hope, one Lord, one faith, one God and Father of all," I can easily bear with their holding wrong opinions, yea, and superstitious modes of worship; nor would I, on these accounts, scruple still to include them within the pale of the catholic Church; neither would I have any objection to receive them, if they desired it, as members of the Church of England.[7]

Albert Outler summarizes Wesley's theology regarding the church as follows:

- The *unity* of the church is based on the Christian *koinonia* in the Holy Spirit.

- The *holiness* of the church is grounded in the discipline of grace which guides and matures the Christian life from its . . . justifying faith to its . . . sanctification.

- The *catholicity* of the church is defined by the universal outreach of redemption, the essential community of all true believers.

- The *apostolicity* of the church is gauged by the succession of apostolic doctrine in those who have been faithful to the apostolic witness.[8]

This seems to be an apt summary. It shows how Wesley took a more charismatic than institutional approach to the church, stressing the vital operations of grace in the life and experience of the believing community.

2. *Wesley's understanding of the church and Christian experience can be described as charismatic because of the place of the Holy Spirit in his theology and because of his openness to the gifts of the Spirit.*

Without debating the precise role of the Holy Spirit in Wesley's doctrine of entire sanctification, or the appropriate terminology to describe the role of the Spirit, we can at least affirm that the Holy Spirit played a significant role in Wesley's thought. Wesley was biblical in understanding salvation in strongly christological rather than primarily pneumatological terms. That is, his primary focus was on Jesus Christ and secondarily on the Holy Spirit. Yet he stressed the Spirit's role in testifying to Christ and making him real to us in present experience. The "more excellent purpose" for which the Holy Spirit was poured out at Pentecost was "to give them . . . the mind which was in Christ, those holy fruits of the Spirit, which whosoever hath not, is none of His."[9]

Wesley did not expound a complete doctrine of the gifts of the Spirit. He did say enough, however (mainly in response to charges that he himself claimed extraordinary gifts and inspirations), for us to understand his general perspective.

He had a fundamental optimism regarding the gifts, though he only occasionally revealed it. He advised Christians that the best gifts "are worth your pursuit, though but few of you can attain them."[10] "Perfecting the saints" in Ephesians 4:12 involves "completing them both in number and their various gifts and graces." Gifts are given for their usefulness, by which "alone are we to estimate all our gifts and talents."[11]

But there is a complicating factor in Wesley's views. He made a distinction between "ordinary" and "extraordinary" gifts that is not precisely biblical and leads to a certain amount of ambiguity in his attitude toward the *charismata*.

The "ordinary gifts" included "convincing speech," persuasion, knowledge, faith, "easy elocution," and pastors and teachers as "ordinary officers."[12] Among the "extraordinary gifts" he included healing, miracles, prophecy (in the sense of foretelling), discernment of spirits, speaking in tongues, and the interpretation of tongues. He describes apostles, prophets, and evangelists as "extraordinary officers." Thus Wesley problematically includes more than the usually identified *charismata* under "ordinary gifts," and he makes a distinction in 1 Corinthians 12 between gifts that are "extraordinary" or "miraculous" and others that are not.[13]

Wesley felt the ordinary gifts were for the church in all ages and should appropriately be desired by Christians—though, of course, governed by love.[14] All the gifts, including the extraordinary ones, had been part of the experience of the church during the first three centuries, he believed, but "even in the infancy of the church, God divided them with a sparing hand," bestowing them principally on those in leadership.[15]

It is important to our discussion to see whether Wesley believed that the extraordinary gifts could be expected in the church in his day. This gives clues as to how he would view the Charismatic renewal of the twentieth century. He writes,

It does not appear that these extraordinary gifts of the Holy Ghost were common in the Church for more than two or three centuries. We seldom hear of them after that fatal period when the Emperor Constantine called himself a Christian. . . . From this time they almost totally ceased; very few instances of the kind were found. The cause of this was not, . . . "because there was no more occasion for them." . . . The real cause was, "the love of many," almost of all Christians, was "waxed cold." . . . This was the real cause why the extraordinary gifts of the Holy Ghost were no longer to be found in the Christian Church.[16]

That the extraordinary gifts were largely inoperative did not mean to Wesley that they had ceased for all time. He believed that God was doing a renewing work through Methodism in his own day. He kept open the possibility of new manifestations of the extraordinary gifts. He felt such gifts either "were designed to remain in the church throughout all ages" or else "they will be restored at the nearer approach of the 'restitution of all things.' "[17]

The extraordinary gifts of the Spirit, according to Wesley, had nearly vanished in his day because of the fallen state of the church. It was not the ideal situation. In fact, God's power was still at work, though hindered by the general coldness and deadness of the church.

Thus Wesley neither encouraged the extraordinary gifts nor disparaged them. He was cautious not to accept too quickly, without significant *ethical* fruit, but he was also careful not to condemn. Consider what he says about his dealings with the "French Prophets" who had come to England from Cevenne in France.

Wesley writes that on January 28, 1739, he "went (having been long importuned thereto) to hear one of the French Prophets, a woman who underwent various convulsions and spoke mostly in words of Scripture." Wesley notes that while some of his companions "believed she spoke by the Spirit of God, this was in no wise clear to me." He adds, "The motion might be either hysterical or artificial. And the same words any person of a good understanding and well versed in the Scriptures might have spoken. But I let the matter alone; knowing this, that 'if it be not of God, it will come to naught.' "[18]

On other occasions Wesley expressed this same cautious attitude toward glossolalia. He wrote, "It seems 'the gift of tongues' was an instantaneous knowledge of a tongue till then unknown, which he that received it could afterwards speak when he thought fit, without any new miracle."[19] He understood tongues as the miraculous ability to speak an actual language, whether previously known or unknown. Because tongues-speaking is a gift of language, God might well not give it "where it would be of no use; as in a Church where all are of one mind, and all speak the same language."[20] But if one possesses the gift of tongues he should "not act so absurdly, as to utter in a congregation what can edify none but" himself. Rather he should speak "that tongue, if he find it profitable to himself in his private devotions."[21]

Is Wesley here referring to a "prayer language" in the modern Pentecostal sense when he makes this rather surprising remark? Probably not, if by this is meant a form of ecstatic utterance bearing no resemblance to known languages. However, he does seem to be allowing for the normal use of a miraculously given ability to use at will, with rational control, a language which the speaker (or pray-er) does not, or previously did not, understand. This comes very close to what many contemporary Charismatics mean by a "prayer language." Contrary to common caricatures, praying in an unknown tongue does not usually mean surrendering control of one's rational faculties. Also, it is interesting that Wesley allows for the use of tongues in private prayer, even though in that case no one but the speaker would be edified.[22]

Wesley's attitude is noteworthy in light of later Pentecostal and Holiness Movement reactions to dramatic behavior. He was an experimentalist, keenly interested in religious experience. His strong emphasis on the rational nature of faith does not mean he would have opposed glossolalia as irrational, for his view of reason was always tempered by experience. He reacted against extreme rationalism as much as against unbiblical "enthusiasm," or fanaticism. He understood that the Christian faith, though rational, also transcends reason. Albert Outler notes,

> Wesley had a remarkably practical rule for judging *extraordinary* gifts of the Spirit (ecstasies, miracles, etc.). . . . No profession of an "extraordinary gift" ("tongues" or whatever) is to be rejected out of hand, as if we knew what the Spirit should or should not do. . . . What he did insist on was that such gifts are never ends in themselves, that all of them must always be normed (and judged) by the Spirit's "ordinary" gifts ("love, joy, peace, patience, kindness, etc., etc.") Like faith, all spiritual gifts are in order to love, which is the measure of all that is claimed to be from God, since God is love.[23]

For Wesley, then, tongues-speaking was subordinate to the law of love. Love is to be preeminent, in the attitudes of both the Charismatic and the noncharismatic critic. We may conjecture that he would take the same moderate attitude toward glossolalia today.

While Wesley's view of spiritual gifts was not developed at length, he was evidently more aware of and more positive toward the *charismata* than most churchmen of his day. This is indicated by his keen interest in all forms of religious experience and by his departure from his source, the German Pietist scholar J. A. Bengel, in his comments on gifts in the *Explanatory Notes*. Wesley often adds observations regarding spiritual gifts that are not found in Bengel. For example, in his comment on 1 Peter 4:10 Wesley employs the ordinary/extraordinary distinction, which Bengel doesn't.[24] Wesley's distinction between ordinary and extraordinary gifts (and offices) did not originate with him, but he took it over and emphasized it.[25]

Partly because of his nonbiblical distinction between ordinary and extraordinary gifts, Wesley failed to see the full, practical significance and necessity of the *charismata* for the life and ministry of the Christian community. We could wish that he had connected ministry in the church more closely with gifts. Except for this reservation, however, we may say that Wesley's theology at this point is charismatic in the New Testament sense.

3. *Wesley's theology is charismatic in its emphasis on the church as community.* Wesley saw that there could be no true church without genuine fellowship. He felt Methodism had a special role to play in encouraging this. Thus he writes in his preface to *Hymns and Sacred Poems* (first edition, 1739),

> It is only when we are knit together that we "have nourishment from Him, and increase with the increase of God." Neither is there any time, when the weakest member can say to the strongest, or the strongest to the weakest, "I have no need of thee." Accordingly our blessed Lord, when His disciples were in their weakest state, sent them forth, not alone, but two by two. When they were strengthened a little, not by solitude, but by abiding with him and one another, he commanded them to "wait," not separate, but "being assembled together," for "the promise of the Father." And "they were all with one accord in one place" when they received the gift of the Holy Ghost. Express mention is made in the same chapter, that when "there were added unto them three thousand souls, all that believed were together, and continued steadfastly" not only "in the Apostles' doctrine," but also "in fellowship and in breaking of bread," and in praying "with one accord."[26]

Wesley goes on to quote from Ephesians 4:12–16 and comments, "The gospel of Christ knows of no religion, but social; no holiness but social holiness."[27] In this instance "social" clearly means "communitary." As this remarkable passage shows, Wesley had a strong and rather untypical sense of the church as community—a view which he learned at least in part from Count Nicholas von Zinzendorf and other Moravians who had discipled him after his conversion.

By Christian fellowship Wesley meant more than merely corporate worship. Fellowship means watching over one another in love; advising, exhorting, admonishing, and praying with the brothers and sisters. "This, and this alone, is Christian fellowship," he said. And this was part of the mission of Methodism: "We introduce Christian fellowship where it was utterly destroyed. And the fruits of it have been peace, joy, love, and zeal for every good word and work."[28] Close community, in other words, helps produce effective ministry.

The great instrument for promoting this quality of community or fellowship was, of course, the Methodist organization: the society, class meeting, and band. For Wesley, the class meeting was an ecclesiological statement, and one integrally linked to Christian perfection. Franklin Littell writes, "Of the various institutions John Wesley introduced to plant and cultivate a living faith, none was so representative of his view of the Christian life as the class meetings. . . ."[29]

Colin Williams adds, "Wesley's view of holiness was woven into his ecclesiology. He believed that the gathering together of believers into small voluntary societies for mutual discipline and Christian growth was essential to the Church's life." He "insisted that there must be *some* form of small group fellowship."[30] In Wesley's view, if believers were really serious in their quest for holiness, they would band together in small groups to experience that level of community which is the necessary environment for growth in grace.[31]

We conclude that Wesley's theology is charismatic from this perspective as well. This charismatic strain puts Wesley's thought in some tension with more recent Wesleyan groups that have wholly abandoned the class meeting or other forms of intimate, accountable group discipleship.

4. *Wesley's theology is charismatic in its tension with institutional expressions of the church.* Here we encounter one of the fundamental tensions in both Wesley's thought and his career. Wesley affirmed the value of the largely decadent institutional church, but he saw Methodism as more truly exhibiting the essential marks of the church. He worked hard to keep the growing Methodist movement within the bounds of the Church of England. This tension between institutional and charismatic tendencies, and this attempt to hold the two together by the animating power of the Spirit within the institution, goes to the very heart of Wesley's concept and practice of the church.

In summary, Wesley's theology is distinctly and fundamentally charismatic, though perhaps not in a fully biblical way. A more adequate biblical view would require rethinking the distinction between the "ordinary" and "extraordinary" gifts, relating gifts more fully and normatively to the various forms of Christian ministry, and giving fuller treatment to the question of the gift of tongues.

PARALLELS BETWEEN METHODISM AND MODERN CHARISMATIC RENEWAL

If Wesley's theology was fundamentally charismatic, does this mean that early Methodism was a Charismatic movement? The parallels between early Methodism and modern Charismatic movements are often striking, particularly when we compare Methodism with movements which, like Methodism, have arisen in fairly traditional liturgical traditions. We may note especially several parallels between early Methodism and contemporary Catholic Charismatic Renewal:

- Both may be described as evangelical movements originating within a largely liturgical-sacramental Catholic tradition;

- Both emphasize personal appropriation and experience of faith in Jesus Christ;

- Both combine the emphases of faith and holiness;

- Both put strong emphasis on singing and praise;

- Both maintain a strong sacramental emphasis, conduct separate meetings for worship and instruction, profess loyalty to the institutional church, claim to be biblical, and stress the role of the Holy Spirit (but not to the detriment of a balanced christological and trinitarian emphasis).

- Both employ a large corps of lay leaders. In fact, early Methodism resembles contemporary Catholic Charismatic Christianity much more than it does Protestant Pentecostal and Charismatic manifestations.

Obviously a major difference between Catholic Charismatic Christianity and Methodism is the place given to the gift of tongues. Other differences are readily identifiable. For example, the Charismatic renewal has no dominant personality who fills the kind of role that John Wesley did in early Methodism. Another difference, worthy of more scrutiny, is that the Charismatic renewal is not so much a movement among the poor as early Methodism was. What does it mean that early Methodism reached the poor masses, whereas the Charismatic renewal—at least in the United States—has not? At this point early Pentecostalism is closer to original Methodism.

A final observation can be made. Even though the gifts of the Spirit played a relatively minor part in

Wesley's theological understanding, their exercise played a major role in the growth of Methodism itself. A key to the Wesleyan system was Wesley's "lay" preachers, whom he considered as exercising a charismatic office. They were people who demonstrated gifts for ministry, and Wesley put them to work, confirming their gifts.

The early Methodist system, in fact, gave broad opportunity for exercising many spiritual gifts. The Methodist societies needed class leaders, band leaders, assistants, stewards, visitors of the sick, and schoolmasters, among others.[32] While these functions were probably not understood primarily as the exercise of spiritual gifts, the whole Methodist system encouraged the kind of spiritual growth in which useful charisms would spring forth and be put into practical service. Methodism provided considerably more opportunity for the exercise of gifts than did the Church of England, where ministry was severely hedged about by clericalism. In this sense Methodist ministry was much more charismatic than Anglican forms of ministry were.

Speaking during a Minister's Week at Emory University, David du Plessis observed,

> While in England recently for a meeting of the Methodist Historical Society, the noted Methodist theologian, Albert Outler, stated that the charismatic movement is not without danger and crudities; but then, neither was early Methodism. "It amazes me a little," he said, "to hear contemporary English Methodism talking about the charismatic renewal in much the same way as the eighteenth century bishop of London talked about the Wesleys and their enthusiasm. . . ."[33]

In light of all these considerations, it is clear that Methodism, at least during Wesley's lifetime, was a charismatic movement in terms of the model we have been using in this book. Later, with the decline of the class meeting, the setting up of Methodist ministerial orders, and the general spiritual decline of the movement, Methodism largely ceased to be charismatic in the biblical sense.

STUDY QUESTIONS

1. We can't escape the period of time in which we live. No doubt John Wesley's beliefs were both influenced and limited by the fact that he lived in the eighteenth century. Even so, how do you think Wesley would react to the Charismatic renewal in the church today?

2. What programs in your church, whether intentionally or not, encourage people to discover and exercise their gifts of grace? What else could be done to encourage and enhance the practice of those gifts?

3. What other similarities or differences do you see in comparing the Methodist Movement with the Charismatic Movement of today?

4. What should be our reaction to unexpected manifestations of spiritual gifts that may occur in our churches? On what basis do we evaluate their legitimacy?

5

WHAT HAPPENED TO THE HOLINESS MOVEMENT?

The American Holiness Movement arose largely in reaction to spiritual decline within Methodism. Its history exhibits some parallels with contemporary Pentecostal and Charismatic Christianity, although perhaps less than original Methodism does. Whereas early Methodism centered in the recovery of the doctrine and experience of the New Birth, the Holiness Movement sprang from a recovery of Wesley's doctrine of entire sanctification as a deeper experience beyond conversion.[1] In this sense, at least, the Holiness Movement has more affinities with modern Charismatic Christianity than early Methodism does.

Viewed from the perspective traced in previous chapters, the Holiness Revival was indeed a charismatic movement. It emphasized grace, the Holy Spirit, and Christian fellowship, and felt keenly the tension between new life and old forms.[2] At least two characteristics of the Holiness Movement were not charismatic, yet prepared the way for modern Pentecostalism. Ironically, both characteristics represented a departure from the breadth and genius of John Wesley.

1. The first characteristic was *a lessened consciousness of Christian community and of the need for structures for community.* We have seen how the class meeting was woven into Wesley's understanding of Christian life and sanctification. It was not for nothing that Wesleyans continued to be called Methodists!

By and large, however, the Holiness Movement failed to perpetuate the intimate, consistent, intense experience of Christian community in the form of the class meeting that was so typical of earlier Methodism. It is true that the Holiness Movement was initially sparked in part by the decline of spirituality and of the class meeting in Methodism, and that small group meetings were one of the keys to the renewal. Wesleyan scholar Melvin Dieter notes,

> The successful use of the small holiness meeting represent-
> ed one positive effort, all unconscious as it may have been,
> to find a substitute to fill the spiritual and social void which
> was being created in the changing Methodist religious
> community by the declining significance of the class meet-
> ing. . . . The Tuesday Meetings and similar holiness meet-
> ings, therefore, fulfilled many of the functions of Wesley's
> "special societies. . . ."
>
> However, in the later movement, gathered together in
> a home as frequently as in a church, and a step removed
> from official pastoral care, . . . they tended to become
> centers of separate interests rather than instruments for
> strengthening the church itself. All that was needed was to
> take the holiness meeting to the masses, and that is
> essentially what the revived camp meeting movement,
> which became the leading edge of the tide of postwar
> holiness revival, was to do.[3]

Dieter's last comment is significant, for it shows a shift that actually led *away* from intimate Christian community at the local level. The holiness camp meeting replaced the class meeting. To a large degree the camp meeting became to the Holiness Movement what the class meeting was to Methodism. By its very nature, however, the camp meeting could not bear the load. Whatever their value, occasional mass gatherings cannot do the job of consistent, weekly, committed cells of seekers after holiness. It could be argued, in fact, that the camp meeting phenomenon tended to shift the perception of the work of holiness from a daily walk with strong ethical implications toward an inner emotional "revival mentality." If so, this is significant both for perceptions of sanctification and for the later development of Pentecostalism.

This is not to say that class meetings died out abruptly or that this was a wholesale shift. We are speaking rather of what seems to have been a gradual but steady trend. Methodist class meetings continued in some places well into the twentieth century, and the Holiness Movement used various forms of small groups, such as Phoebe Palmer's "Tuesday Meetings." But it is clear that during the last half of the nineteenth century the class meeting was in decline while the camp meeting was in ascendancy.[4]

Charles W. Ferguson identifies this as a broad trend in Methodism in *Organizing to Beat the Devil: Methodists and the Making of America:*

> At first the Methodists [in the U.S.] struck a balance between the camp meetings and the class meetings. In this combination the mini and the mass joined. But when camp assemblies became a sustaining feature in Methodist practice, group meetings subsided and fell gradually into disuse. Many undetermined factors may have entered into the change, but the fact is that the growth of mass efforts during the years before 1805 and 1844 coincided with a shrinking of group activities.
>
> Methodism moved toward the mass rather than the group as the primary form in society.[5]

The Holiness Movement, like U.S. Methodism generally, put less stress on fellowship and community at the local level than did earlier Methodism. One consequence of this was less opportunity for the practical exercise of spiritual gifts on a broad scale.

2. A second development in the Holiness Movement was *a narrowing of John Wesley's conception of Christian perfection.* A careful reading of Wesley's sermons will show that the fundamental strain in Wesley's doctrine of sanctification is that of process: growing up into the fullness of Christ; attaining the mind of Christ and the image of God; loving God with one's soul, strength, and mind. To this Wesley added, on the basis of experience and seemingly by analogy with his understanding of the New Birth, his doctrine of a second crisis experience in which the believer is entirely sanctified, cleansed, and empowered to love God and others fully, as God intends, without hindrance from an impure "heart."

The Holiness Movement in the nineteenth century stressed the second crisis and deemphasized sanctification as a process of growth that begins with conversion and continues through life. Moreover, the broader context and structure of Wesley's overall theology was largely lost from sight. Holiness came to be seen primarily as a state of being. Thus Seth Cook Rees could write in 1897, "Holiness is a state; entire sanctification is an experience; the Holy Ghost is a person. We come into the state of holiness through the experience of entire sanctification, wrought by the omnipotent energies of the Holy Ghost."[6] Admittedly this "state" was a state of growth, but the accent had shifted.

With this shift in emphasis came, as several scholars have shown, a shift toward pneumatological language and an increased emphasis on the baptism of the Holy Spirit. These two developments—no doubt influenced by other trends in U.S. society in the late nineteenth century—tended to produce an un-Wesleyan pessimism toward the expected norms for personal and corporate

Christian experience. The Holiness Movement tended to stress a series of peak experiences which were seen as carrying the believer through the low points in between. The absence of consistent structures designed to help people grow in sanctification (such as the class meeting) reinforced this psychology.

On these two points, at least, the Holiness Movement was less biblically charismatic than was early Methodism and yet was moving toward modern Pentecostalism. In Wesley's view, the earnest Christian is always growing in sanctification. The second crisis is important, but more as a means than as a goal. By contrast, the Holiness Movement increasingly tended to see the second crisis as the goal of Christian experience, the end to which all prior growth in grace tends.[7] For example, Melvin Dieter notes that Phoebe Palmer's doctrine of entire sanctification, compared with Wesley's, "greatly enhanced the distinctiveness of the second blessing from that of the initial experience of regeneration." The result of such tendencies, says Dieter, "was that the American holiness revival came to emphasize crisis stages of salvation at the expense of an emphasis on growth in grace."[8]

From this perspective, Holiness theology in the late nineteenth century logically leads either to Pentecostalism or to some disillusionment with the second crisis experience. By its very nature, a spiritual peak experience cannot be permanently satisfying. If that occasion is a genuine experience of the Holy Spirit in His fullness (which we do not question), we would expect that the daily presence of the Spirit in the believer's life would be fully satisfying—and that *was* the expectation. But without normative structures for nurturing the life of holiness, and with the increasing stress on subjective crises typified by the growing use of Pentecostal crisis language,[9] many Holiness people no doubt felt an inner lack in their lives, a sense that there must be something deeper, something more, in Christian experience. So then, after the turn of the century the question logically became, could this "something more" be the new phenomenon of speaking in tongues? Many concluded that it was. Other groups staunchly resisted this new Pentecostalism, and on that issue the Holiness Movement divided.[10]

These developments in the late-nineteenth-century Holiness Movement lead us to two conclusions:

1. *The fully Wesleyan understanding of Christian perfection, combining both process and crisis, must be recovered.* This is the biblical view. In fact, the main question before us is not whether Spirit-baptism language is appropriate. The more basic question is this: How do we in fact teach, encourage, and make structural provision for the life of "all inward and outward holiness"? There is a biblical and practical breadth to the Wesleyan understanding of Christian experience that must be recovered in our day. In this area the Holiness Movement would be more dynamic if it were more Wesleyan.

2. *In this light, modern Pentecostalism may be viewed in both positive and negative ways.* Positively, Pentecostalism in both its classical and newer Charismatic forms has recovered and extended much of the spiritual dynamism of the older Holiness Movement. It has been responsible, under God, for millions of people on all continents coming to know Jesus Christ as Savior and Lord. Whether Wesleyans like it or not, in some sense the mantle of the Holiness Movement as a spiritual revitalizing force has passed to the Pentecostal and Charismatic movements, which have had a much greater impact than our own tradition in our day.

Furthermore, the Pentecostal and Charismatic movements have raised the question of the *charismata* and the question of the charismatic nature of Christianity in a way that has forced the church at large to reexamine what the Scriptures say on this subject. The growing consciousness throughout the church of the practical dimensions of the *charismata* is directly traceable to modern Pentecostalism (and indirectly to Wesleyanism).

Negatively, Pentecostalism and to some degree the Charismatic Movement have not yet recovered the ethical, spiritual, and social depth and breadth of early Methodism. In some sectors the sanctifying emphasis has not been sufficiently retained. Stress on the more dramatic gifts has not always been accompanied by a sufficiently balanced emphasis on the fruit of the Spirit and the social impact of the gospel. More balance in this area now seems evident in some branches of the Pentecostal and Charismatic movements, and especially in the Catholic Charismatic Renewal.

In any case, the Holiness reaction to Pentecostalism and Neo-Pentecostalism has been too harsh. Vinson Synan notes,

> The most negative assessments of the [modern Charismatic] renewal came from the older Holiness and fundamentalist churches that had encountered and rejected Pentecostalism earlier in the century. . . . Nazarenes rejected the renewal out of hand, not on scriptural or theological grounds, but because Pentecostalism did not accord with their doctrines and traditions.[11]

Unfortunately, this has been true of most non-Pentecostal Holiness groups.

Given the historical circumstances, it is understandable that many in the Holiness Movement resisted the outbreak of Pentecostalism, denouncing the gift of tongues with the same vehemence of Pentecostals who promoted it. The more tongues became the focal point of Pentecostalism, the more it became the lightning rod of Holiness opposition. This is a familiar pattern at the outbreak of new movements. The unfortunate result is that often in such a circumstance, the old movement is left without the dynamic of the new and the new is left without the stability and balance of the old.

But now we are in a new period. The Pentecostal and Charismatic movements are here to stay. Indeed, in some sectors these movements are showing signs of institutionalism and accommodation. Conversely, Holiness bodies are gradually softening their opposition to Pentecostal and Charismatic themes and are beginning to take a second look. It is time to build bridges of understanding and to ask how the Holy Spirit might be pleased to build in this day a church that is charismatic and holy in a truly biblical way.

In doing so we would fulfill the vision of that great Methodist missionary to America, Francis Asbury, who wrote in his journal in 1786: "I feel the worth of souls, and the weight of the pastoral charge, and that the conscientious discharge of its important duties requires something more than human learning, unwieldy salaries, or clerical titles of D.D., or even *bishop*. The eyes of all—both preachers and people, will be opened in time."[12]

STUDY QUESTIONS

1. What do Charismatic churches today have to learn from churches of the Holiness tradition?

2. What can churches of the Holiness tradition learn from the Charismatic renewal?

3. Moses felt the weight of leadership so greatly that he sighed, "Oh that all God's people could be filled with the Holy Spirit." Francis Asbury must have felt the same way when he wrote the journal entry quoted at the end of this chapter. Yet Asbury lived seventeen hundred years after Pentecost. The Holy Spirit had already been given to the church centuries before.

What accounts for the relative absence of the gifts of grace in the life of the church down through history?

4. Does your church have any structures resembling the old Methodist class meeting? What can be done in your church today to restore or deepen the sense of community and accountability of the class meeting?

6

A CONTEMPORARY AGENDA

Where does the foregoing analysis leave contemporary Wesleyan Christians? It suggests three major considerations that should be part of the agenda for Wesleyans as we confront and interact with Charismatic Christianity.

1. *We should reevaluate our arguments in opposition to Pentecostalism in general and the gifts of the Spirit in particular.*
Most Wesleyan commentators, conscious of history and of the similarity at certain points of Wesleyan and Pentecostal theology, have understandably approached the question of spiritual gifts from a defensive and apologetic viewpoint, rather than from a positive and constructive one. Our primary concern has been to explain why we differ from Pentecostals and to defend our ranks against outbreaks of tongues-speaking. Most of the Wesleyan-Holiness literature on gifts has therefore had this negative and defensive character.[1]

More recently, some Wesleyans have begun to approach the question of gifts in a broader and more constructive way. They are asking how a proper biblical understanding of gifts can make us more effective in our work and witness. Two books with similar titles exemplify these two approaches within Wesleyan-Holiness ranks: W. T. Purkiser's *Gifts of the Spirit* and Kenneth C. Kinghorn's *Gifts of the Spirit*. Purkiser takes care to guard against glossolalia, while Kinghorn is more open to all the gifts.

Most Holiness writing on the gifts so far has zeroed in on tongues-speaking, focusing particularly on the Corinthian problem. The general line of reasoning has been similar to that described by Charles Hummel in his book, *Fire in the Fireplace:*

> Most commentaries paint a picture of [speaking in tongues] along the following lines: at Corinth it was an emotional, sensational experience similar to the ecstasy of the pagan religions. The Christians had an exaggerated respect for this gift which they considered of the highest value. Misuse of tongues was the greatest problem in the church. Paul considers it of least value since it appears last on some of his lists. At best he begrudgingly commands that it not be forbidden.[2]

As Hummel notes, there are several logical and hermeneutical problems with this approach. He comments,

> Paul's statements do not support these conjectures. Significantly, these opinions come from a culture for which speaking in tongues is both intellectually and socially unacceptable. Since in every generation Christianity is influenced by its environment, is it not possible that this spiritual gift is far more a problem for the modern church than it was for the Corinthians? The first eleven chapters of I Corinthians indicate that for Paul other issues were of much greater concern.[3]

Strictly from the standpoint of logic, some of the most common arguments against glossolalia must be questioned. This does not mean that glossolalia should be promoted or permitted without restriction, that every outbreak of "tongues" is legitimate or authentic, or that there are no cogent arguments against the practice. But it does suggest some need for reevaluation on the part of

Wesleyans. We might well heed Kenneth Kinghorn's admonition to avoid both "charismania" and "charisphobia" in dealing with the gifts.

In the case against speaking in tongues, for example, a sharp distinction is often made between tongues as the miraculous speaking of a known but unlearned language and *glossolalia* as an "unknown tongue" or ecstatic speech. But this distinction is not so obvious and logical as it seems.

First, the New Testament does not make or support this distinction, although it is clear that known languages were involved at least on the Day of Pentecost. While different kinds of tongues-speaking seem to be reported in the New Testament, no biblical writer makes the language/nonlanguage distinction that is common today, at least not as a way of validating the one and condemning the other. The issue in 1 Corinthians 14 is not *what* is spoken but *when* it is spoken and whether the congregation is edified through interpretation. In Acts 2 we know for sure that a variety of known languages was spoken; we do not know whether "unknown tongues" were also manifested. Apparently that was not an important question to Luke.

Second, the idea that nonlanguage tongues-speaking is a highly emotional, irrational, ecstatic form of behavior involving "mindless utterances"[4] or being "out of control"[5] is a caricature that most Charismatics would reject.

Third, it is not clear that it makes any real psychological or spiritual difference to tongues-speakers whether they are uttering a "known" or "unknown" tongue if in any case the tongue is unknown to them. In either case, to them it is an "unknown tongue" that is in some sense unintelligible.

Another logical problem is the inconsistency of the arguments made against tongues. One writer, for instance, considers tongues-speaking (other than known languages) as illegitimate because it involves yielding one's rational control to an irrational, overpowering, ecstatic speech pattern. Another author argues that tongues can't be legitimate because the speaker can speak in tongues deliberately at will, whereas a truly valid spiritual gift comes by the direct inspiration of the Holy Spirit.[6] One argues that tongues is wrong because it is irrational and uncontrollable; the other that it is false because it is rationally controllable!

The truth, however, would appear to be that tongues-speaking is a nonrational but not necessarily irrational speech pattern which lies within the range of normal human behavior. Such tongues-speaking may or may not be prompted or inspired by the Holy Spirit. In some contexts it may be induced by other forces, whether psychological, social, or demonic. This is no more than we would admit for other rather extraordinary forms of behavior which in certain contexts we do not consider abnormal or pathological, including crying, screaming, shouting, or dancing. In this sense, "getting blessed" has many parallels to tongues-speaking. Sometimes it may be of the Spirit; other times it is clearly a manifestation of "the flesh."

Probably the major argument against glossolalia in Holiness circles has been that it is an irrational form of behavior and speech, while the gospel always calls us to rational behavior and speech.[7] This argument needs reevaluation on at least two counts. First, it operates on the basis of an unnecessary rational/irrational dichotomy or polarity. What is not totally rational to us may not be irrational; it may simply be nonrational (in the sense that emotions in general, for instance, are nonrational but not by definition irrational). Or it may simply function beyond our present level of knowledge. Thus we now know Einstein's theory of relativity is not irrational, although it appeared to be so at first. In this sense, tongues-speaking when accompanied by other signs of the work of the Spirit—notably the fruit of the Spirit—may have its own reason and rationality that we have yet been unable to fully discern.[8]

The second problem with this argument against tongues-speaking is its assumption that modern glossolalia is a highly emotional, ecstatic experience, verging on frenzy, as in pagan religions. But this is an unfair caricature. Hummel notes,

> Since some pagan religions have a glossolalia involving frenzy and trance, it is often assumed that the Christian experience is similar. These religions also have ordinary prayer, meditation and sacrifice, but their meaning is hardly determinative for the Christian expression. On the contrary, the Corinthians were not possessed by evil spirits but were led by the Holy Spirit. In fact Paul assumed that they could control their speaking in tongues (14:24).
>
> The Corinthians may have exercised this gift with strong emotion, just as they may have prayed, prophesied or sung emotionally. But this style of expression is not inherent in the gift.[9]

The real danger in a negative approach to tongues, however, is that it may lead to the hyperrationalism of dead orthodoxy. Wesleyans, of all people, should be open to the working of God in human experience. We should be wary of stating in advance how the Spirit shall or shall not operate. We should maintain the balance of reason, experience, and Scripture that characterized John Wesley.

We may criticize some Pentecostals for making tongues the necessary evidence of the fullness of the Spirit or for attempting to induce people to seek or experience this gift. But we should be careful that our arguments grow inductively from Scripture and stand the test of the rationality for which we contend.[10] The modern Wesleyan polemic against tongues has been grounded in an appeal to reason. But the arguments have not been totally sound, especially when viewed in the light of the apostle Paul's letters to the church at Corinth.

The most difficult passages for a rigid anti-tongues position, as some Wesleyan writers have noted, are three of Paul's statements in 1 Corinthians 14:

— "I would like every one of you to speak in tongues" (v. 5);
— "I thank God that I speak in tongues more than all of you" (v. 18);
— "Do not forbid speaking in tongues" (v. 39).

Some Wesleyan writers and others have gone to great lengths in attempting to establish that these statements do not mean what they seem to say (even suggesting that Paul is employing a very subtle psychological method here). However, a sound hermeneutic demands that we take these statements and the whole chapter at face value and in as straightforward a manner as possible. Such an approach must take note of several things:

a. There is no sound exegetical basis in 1 Corinthians 14 for giving "tongues" two different meanings in Paul's use here or for restricting "tongues" to "known language." Whatever Paul means when he speaks of Corinthian tongues-speaking, he means the same thing when he speaks of his own experience.

b. Paul's affirmation that "I speak in tongues more than all of you" cannot, by the text or context, be required to mean "I speak in more languages than all of you." First, in the following verse Paul contrasts his own tongues-speaking with "intelligible words," which would seem to mean that he in fact knew something about speaking in nonintelligible words. Second, the context here is the *gift* of tongues, not the acquired ability to speak languages. Even if "tongues" in verse 18 means "languages," the interpretation would have to be, "I thank God that I miraculously speak in languages I never learned more than all of you." But there is no more biblical support for the idea that Paul in fact frequently employed Spirit-inspired, unlearned known languages in his ministry than there is that he spoke in "unknown tongues." So the question must be left open.

c. Paul's statement "I would like every one of you to speak in tongues" cannot with consistency be understood as an encouragement to speak in various known languages unless verse 2 is understood as saying "anyone who speaks in a known language speaks only to God"— which makes little sense.

d. Similarly, in the context of the whole chapter, verse 39 means literally what it says: Do not forbid tongues-speaking! Whatever the nature of the tongues-speaking going on in Corinth, Paul says: Do not forbid it (or possibly, "Stop forbidding it").[11] Control it according to the teaching of this chapter, yes; but do not forbid. This is the "bottom line" of the teaching in this chapter.

In addition, note the positive things Paul clearly *does* say about tongues-speaking at Corinth:

— The person who speaks in tongues speaks to God (v. 2);
— "He who speaks in a tongue edifies himself" (v. 4; there is no suggestion that it is wrong for a believer personally to be edified in this way);
— Tongues-speaking, if interpreted, is just as important and edifying as prophecy (v. 5);
— Speaking in tongues is of help to a congregation if it is accompanied by "some revelation or knowledge or prophecy or word of instruction" (v. 6);
— The one speaking in tongues "utters mysteries with his spirit" or "by the Spirit" (v. 2; no criticism is implied per se, but only as this relates to public worship);
— when people speak in tongues, their spirits are praying (v. 14; again, no criticism is implied).

First Corinthians 14 was Paul's (and the Spirit's) perfect opportunity to put a stop to glossolalia once and for all. But Paul did not do this. Clearly, he saw the dangers of a total prohibition and was satisfied merely to state general restrictions in the interest of good order in public worship.

We realize that some may consider the degree of openness to Pentecostalism suggested in these pages to be an encouragement of tongues-speaking. This is not our intent. These comments are made only in the interest of an interpretation of Scripture that is logically sound and hermeneutically faithful, and out of concern that we not limit the work of the Spirit in the church. The most balanced policy seems to be the same as that of Wesley and mid-nineteenth-century Holiness leaders toward strong emotional manifestations: "Do not encourage; do not forbid; judge by the fruit."

The evidence suggests that we in the Wesleyan tradition should become more open toward and work more closely with our many Christian sisters and brothers in Charismatic groups. We should appreciate the work God is doing through them. They can learn from us, and we can learn from them.

2. *We should understand what the Charismatic Movement is today.* Many common perceptions simply do not stand up to the facts. For example, the movement is much more diverse than often painted. We find not only the historical distinction between the older Pentecostalism and the newer Charismatic renewal, but also widespread varieties and differences within both. The more recent Charismatic renewal may be divided generally into the Catholic Charismatic Renewal, the Charismatic Movement within the mainline denominations, the somewhat nebulous group associated with The 700 Club and The PTL Club, old-line Pentecostalists who have "made the switch" to

the newer Charismatic style, and the rather close-knit group associated with Bob Mumford, Charles Simpson, Ern Baxter, and others. Also, there are now fairly well-organized Charismatic renewal movements in some smaller, more-or-less evangelical denominations, such as the Mennonite Charismatic Renewal. There have also been modest attempts to initiate a Wesleyan Charismatic fellowship. A small conference was held for this purpose in Cincinnati in January 1979.

These groups vary more widely than many people realize. They differ in their understanding of the precise role of tongues-speaking in Christian experience and in the church, although they all practice tongues-speaking. Many do not hold that tongues are a necessary evidence of being filled with the Spirit. Also, tongues are generally not the main concern of Charismatic groups that have been around for a decade or more. Many Charismatic groups are now primarily concerned with questions of Christian community building, discipling, authority, family life, and personal spiritual growth. To put it another way, there is a growing concern with ethical questions. One need not agree with Pentecostal and Charismatic interpretations of tongues (as we generally do not) to appreciate the diversity and spiritual vitality in much of the movement.

Nowhere do common stereotypes of the Charismatic Movement become more inappropriate than when we examine the Catholic Charismatic Renewal. Here is a movement that is very conscious of historic Christian roots and of the call to a life of holiness. A review of several issues of *New Covenant* magazine or the more recent publication *Pastoral Renewal* will show the blending of evangelical and Catholic emphases that marks the Catholic Charismatic Renewal. As noted earlier, the Catholic Charismatic Renewal has many parallels with eighteenth-century Methodism (as well as many differ-

ences), and there is no reason why contemporary Wesleyans should not have frequent and close fellowship with
this branch of the Body of Christ.[12]

3. Finally, *we should seek a more biblically charismatic
expression of the church.*

We have already indicated the general direction this
concern should take. We must seek to be charismatic in
the fully biblical sense. Among other things, this means:

- A new awareness of the possibilities and potential
  of God's grace in human experience, the church,
  and in society. We need to recover John Wesley's
  optimism of grace as seen, for example, in his
  sermon, "The General Spread of the Gospel."

- A rediscovery of the charismatic nature and structure of the church. This means a balanced emphasis on gifts, but it also means understanding that
  the *charismata* provide a foundational insight for
  understanding the varieties of ministry within the
  church. We need to combine an emphasis on gifts
  with a reaffirmation of the doctrine of the priesthood of all believers. This recognizes that all
  believers are called to the servant-ministry
  (*diakonia*) of Jesus Christ.

- A recovery of the understanding and experience of
  the church as community. We need to see and
  experience the church primarily as a charismatic
  organism, rather than as an institutional organization. This means recovering some functional equiv-
  alent of the class meeting, but it also means a much
  deeper understanding of the nature of New Testament *koinonia*.

- A fully charismatic expression of the church that
  understands itself as a proto-community of the

kingdom of God. This implies seeking by God's grace to be a messianic expression of the kingdom in a world of contrary values. Perhaps no Wesleyan thinker in modern times has seen this more clearly than has E. Stanley Jones.[13]

- A charismatic expression of the church that in no way compromises the call to sanctity and holiness. Rather, it will see holiness as encompassing both the corporate and individual experience of believers, and it will see the Christian community as the essential environment for making progress in the life of holiness. It will be concerned with the sanctification of the Body of Christ (Eph. 4:14–16; 5:27).

- An awareness that the life and witness of the church stem from the work of the Holy Spirit. A biblically charismatic church will seek to manifest the "catholic spirit" that John Wesley advocated.[14] It will seek visible expression of the unity of the church, basing that unity on openness and sensitivity toward the working of the Holy Spirit in the various branches of Christendom.

STUDY QUESTIONS

1. Why has the practice of tongues-speaking been objectionable to Wesleyan Christians in times past? Has this been due to an overemphasis on tongues by Pentecostals and Charismatics?

2. How can Wesleyans and Charismatics work to minimize their differences and focus instead on their common Christian beliefs and calling?

3. Once achieved, what might be the result of a greater sense of unity and purpose between Wesleyans and Charismatics?

7

THE DIALOGUE BEGINS

In 1943 several American Pentecostal denominations were invited to join the National Association of Evangelicals. This marked perhaps the first time in church history that Charismatic groups were accepted into a major transdenominational Christian body. It is worth noting that several Wesleyan groups were active in forming the NAE and that the association's first president, Leslie R. Marston, was a Free Methodist bishop.

Rapid growth of Pentecostal churches and the increasing prosperity of Pentecostals after the Second World War probably contributed to this growing acceptance. Vinson Synan asserts that these events, plus the influence of such programs as the Full Gospel Businessmen's Fellowship International and the advent of Oral Roberts' television ministry in the early sixties, set the stage for widespread recognition and acceptance of the modern Charismatic Movement.[1]

As early as the fifties, constructive dialogue was underway between the Pentecostal movement and mainline Protestant denominations. Churches involved in the ecumenical movement, especially, began to recognize the *charismata* in all their manifestations as a legitimate Christian expression. This positive dialogue has continued through the development of the Charismatic renewal of the sixties and seventies.[2]

In the last two decades many church groups have taken steps to make peace with the growing Neo-Pentecostal Movement. Several denominations issued guarded pronouncements of acceptance and recognition of the significance of the Charismatic renewal. These included the Lutheran Church in America,[3] the Presbyterian Church in the United States,[4] and the United Presbyterian Church, U.S.A.[5]

The United Presbyterian report is particularly insightful in that it "requests tolerance on the part of ministers, sessions, and presbyteries toward Neo-Pentecostalism in their churches; urges that *charismata* always be practiced 'decently and in order' (the Pauline injunction); and expresses its approval of the renewing work of the Holy Spirit wherever such activity is to be found."[6] The United Presbyterian Church's guidelines on how to deal with Pentecostal phenomena may also be useful to churches in the Wesleyan tradition:

1. Be tolerant and accepting of those whose Christian experiences differ from your own;

2. Continually undergird and envelop all discussions, conferences, meetings, and persons in prayer;

3. Be open to new ways in which God by his Spirit may be speaking to the Church;

4. Recognize that even though spiritual gifts may be abused, this does not mean that they should be prohibited;

5. Remember that like other new movements in church history, Neo-Pentecostalism may have a valid contribution to make to the ecumenical Church.[7]

A Committee on Doctrine appointed by the Roman Catholic bishops of the United States also concluded that the Charismatic (Neo-Pentecostal) Movement should "not be inhibited but allowed to develop," and indicated in its report that "theologically the movement has legitimate reasons for existence. It has a strong biblical basis."[8]

The evangelical community, theologically closer to the Pentecostals than mainline ecumenical Christians, has made hesitant but sincere attempts at reconciliation, as indicated in an editorial in *Eternity* in 1973:

> More and more evangelical scholars today feel that the traditional, supposed biblical arguments for the cessation of the gifts after completion of the New Testament, cannot be sustained by the Holy Scriptures.
>
> The new stress is on the church as the body of Christ with its various members endowed by the Spirit with differing gifts. The gifts are "apportioned to each of us as the Spirit chooses" (1 Cor. 12:11, Goodspeed). And who would rule out tongues as one of these gifts? Certainly Paul didn't.[9]

Equally significant, in 1969 *Christianity Today*, perhaps the most influential periodical in evangelical circles, advocated tolerance toward Christians who speak in tongues.[10] Harold Lindsell, a former editor of *Christianity Today*, has stated,

> I accept as a fact that some of God's people are filled or baptized with the Holy Spirit, and that nomenclature is purely a secondary matter that should not keep us from appropriating what lies behind differing terms for the same experience. It is also a fact that God, through His Spirit, does perform miracles and healings. Speaking in tongues does happen and is a bona fide gift of the Spirit. . . . These gifts have not ceased.[11]

Vinson Synan comments on these developments, particularly with reference to the Methodist tradition:

Although the roots of the renewal in some ways lay in the Methodist tradition, the United Methodist Church belatedly produced its first major evaluation of the movement in 1976. While noting that Pentecostalism had emerged from the Wesleyan tradition, the report stated that Pentecostalism "has little to do with Wesley's theology."

Nevertheless, tongues-speakers were welcomed in Methodist churches, as was dramatically demonstrated in 1969 when Oral Roberts was admitted to the Boston Avenue Methodist Church in Tulsa, Oklahoma. Roberts was also admitted as a local preacher in the Oklahoma Conference by Bishop Angie Smith after promising the bishop and his thousands of "partners" that he would change neither his pentecostal theology nor his divine healing methods. The Graduate School of Theology of Oral Roberts University, headed by Methodist theologian Dr. Jimmy Buskirk, was approved by the United Methodist Church in 1982 as a seminary for the training of Methodist ministers.[12]

These developments do not suggest unequivocal or uncritical acceptance of the *charismata* in all forms, but they do at least indicate a willingness to hold constructive dialogue. One notable exception would be the staunchly dispensational groups which continue to insist that the *charismata* disappeared following the apostolic era and that any such phenomena today are counterfeit or even satanic.

More legitimate and discerning appraisals of Pentecostal experience are now coming from evangelical and Holiness groups. John Stott, the respected Church of England evangelical, makes this mild criticism of Pentecostal and Charismatic theology—which, incidentally, could equally be seen as a criticism of the Wesleyan teaching on entire sanctification:

It is spiritual *graces* which should be common to all Christians, not spiritual *gifts* or spiritual *experiences*. The gifts of the Spirit are distributed among different Christians (I Cor. 12); it is the fruit of the Spirit which should characterize all. . . . I would appeal to you not to urge upon people a baptism with the Spirit as a second and subsequent experience entirely distinct from conversion, for this cannot be proved from Scripture.[13]

Wesleyans will not fully agree with Stott here, any more than Pentecostals will. Both gifts *and* graces are given to all believers, according to the New Testament. Often the Spirit does cleanse and empower believers in a distinct experience subsequent to conversion—whatever their theology.

SUMMARY

In general, a trend away from opposition and toward acceptance (and even approval) of the many new manifestations of the *charismata* seems to be growing in the church. Some Pentecostal and Charismatic leaders see this acceptance as the beginning of a "third wave" of Pentecostalism. The first wave came early in this century; the second wave followed Vatican II. The third wave, it is said, will consist of Pentecostal experience quietly entering mainline churches with little opposition as evangelicals in traditional churches seek, receive, and exercise the gifts of the Spirit, though without accepting "Pentecostal" or "Charismatic" labels.

To some extent this kind of leavening is already happening. Peter Wagner of Fuller Theological Seminary writes,

> I see myself as neither a Charismatic nor a Pentecostal. I belong to the Lake Avenue Congregational Church. . . . My church is not a charismatic church, although some of our members are charismatic. There is a charismatic prayer group. . . . Our pastor gives an invitation after every service for people who need physical healing and inner healing. . . . We have teams of people who know how to pray for the sick. We like to think that we are doing it in a congregational way; we're not doing it in a charismatic way. But we're getting the same results.[14]

Of course, this will not happen in churches until it starts happening in the lives of individuals. One example is related by Anglican pastor George Carey. He tells about a rigid Reformed man in his congregation whose narrow Christianity permitted him to fellowship only with like-minded people. Carey writes,

> But his life changed in a remarkable way. He went to the United States on a lecture tour, and he met a group of charismatic Christians who led him into an experience of the Holy Spirit that revolutionized his theology. No longer narrow, this man is an open Christian, expressing great joy and love in a liberated life. His love of the Bible is just as great as before, and his hold on biblical doctrines such as justification by faith is just as strong. But his charismatic experience is a bridge which has brought him closer to other Christians.[15]

This type of experience is not unusual today. Carey comments, "Theological dialog is, of course, important and must continue, but at the grassroots level the Spirit is moving and already taking many Christians to a level of spiritual unity far deeper than the union of ecclesiastical bodies."[16]

Wesleyans have a choice. God seems to be restoring his gifts to the church today in considerable magnitude. Will Wesleyans respond with greater openness to the Spirit's gifts? Or will they maintain the stalemate that has divided most Wesleyans from their Pentecostal and Charismatic sisters and brothers for decades?

STUDY QUESTIONS

1. It's interesting that Presbyterian, Lutheran, and Catholic churches have been more open to Charismatic renewal than have some evangelical churches which are theologically closer to Pentecostals and Charismatics. Why is this the case?

2. What do Evangelicals stand to gain by embracing the Charismatic Movement as a legitimate expression of the church?

3. Peter Wagner says his church practices the gifts of grace but does so "in a congregational way, not in a charismatic way." If the exercise of charismatic gifts is part of your church life, has this changed the church's doctrine or organization in any way? If your church does not practice such gifts, could they be a part of your church's life without being disruptive to doctrine or organization?

4. Never in church history has there been such emphasis on the gifts of grace as today, or so much acceptance of the *charismata* by church authorities. Because of this new openness, dramatic changes are possible, and likely. Try to picture your own church and community ten years from now. What changes will have occurred by then if the gifts of grace are freely exercised?

5. Joel prophesied, "In the last days, God says, I will pour out my Spirit on all people . . ." (see Joel 2:28–32 and Acts 2:16–21). Although this has happened here and there throughout the history of the church, it appears to be happening on a larger scale in the twentieth century. Would you draw any conclusions about the Charismatic Movement based on this observation?

6. What do you think accounts for the greater emphasis on, and acceptance of, spiritual gifts today?

8

PASTORAL GUIDELINES

Those who occupy responsible places in the structures of
churches, schools, and denominations wonder what will
happen when an outpouring of the Spirit comes. They are
tempted to ask, "What will this outpouring do to our
organization?" "What will our donors think?" "What will
the literature the spiritual enthusiasts write do to our
denominational circulations?" "What if these enthusiasts
create a new church, splitting congregations into warring
factions?"[1]

In the course of church history, many renewal
movements have been condemned as heretical. However,
some renewal movements have remained in the church,
successfully leavening its life and witness. Examples in
Catholic history include the ascetic movement of the
fourth century, the Cluniac reformers in the eleventh
century, the mendicant movement associated with Inno-
cent III in the thirteenth century, and the Oxford Movement among Anglicans and Catholics in the nineteenth
century. Many of the Catholic orders were renewal and
reform movements in their initial stages. The most
graphic examples in Protestant history are the evangelical
awakenings of the eighteenth and nineteenth centuries,
but many others could be cited.[2]

HOW TO BE WESLEYAN AND CHARISMATIC

Today's Charismatic renewal offers a special challenge to noncharismatic churches because of its pervasive presence. Almost every church tradition—Catholic, Anglican, Orthodox, Reformed, Anabaptist, Holiness, Pentecostal—is experiencing some degree of Charismatic leavening and new awareness of the *charismata*. In its call for dialogue and understanding, particularly on the part of Wesleyans, this book would be incomplete without suggesting some ways this can be accomplished.

The Roman Catholic Church has formally recognized Charismatic renewal as a positive and constructive force. Some of their efforts toward integrating the renewal movement could also be successfully adapted by Protestant churches.

One Catholic approach has been to allow Charismatic prayer groups to relate to the parish in the same way as other parish organizations, with a priest or chaplain participating only at crisis moments and ceremonial events. A second technique is to appoint a bishop's representative to the movement as is done for other lay movements. A third approach is for priests to participate actively in the renewal, both as leaders and as participants.[3] Protestant parallels to these three ideas might include:

- Scheduling Charismatic prayer meetings and recognizing them as official church functions;

- Designating a responsible church leader to "shepherd" the Charismatic renewal within each church. When the demand is great enough, perhaps an officer or bishop in the church headquarters could accept responsibility to provide leadership and guidance to a denomination-wide Charismatic emphasis;

- Encouraging pastors to participate actively in the renewal, as leaders or participants, and providing them with the necessary training and materials to help them integrate the renewal into regular church functions.

Stephen Clark has studied the ascetic movement of the fourth century in some detail and notes marked similarities to the modern Charismatic renewal. By examining the pastoral steps taken by church leaders of that day, he has discovered several principles that can be followed to successfully incorporate the renewal's spiritual vitality into church life today. Although the language is oriented toward Catholic leadership, the principles apply to Protestants as well:

- The unordained elder is an important figure in the tradition of the Church, not an abuse: having unordained elders allows pastoral flexibility and innovation, especially in a new or changing situation.

- The normal way for a renewal community to be related to the Church as a whole is by the ordination of its leader(s) to the presbyterate of the diocese in which the community is situated.

- The renewal community should be drawn upon to make an important contribution to the pastoral strength and the ordained leadership of the Church as a whole.[4]

Clark is calling here for what several Protestant renewal leaders have in fact done—using and recognizing those with maturity and gifts to assist in the life and equipping of the whole congregation. Philip Jacob Spener in Germany championed this in 1675, in effect launching the Pietist Movement, and Wesley accomplished essentially the same thing through his network of "lay" preachers and class leaders.

Giving Charismatic leaders recognition and responsibility within the local church or the denomination is vital because of the community nature of the Charismatic Movement. Of course, such steps must be taken carefully and with some accountability built in. Normally a community is more comfortable choosing its own leaders rather than having a leader assigned to it by someone outside. When Charismatic leaders are not given recognition and responsibility, the usual result is conflict and division. Often this leads to the establishment of yet another church or denomination—which tends to flourish while the parent church stagnates.

Charismatic leaders who break away from their mother church often do so involuntarily and reluctantly. In most cases they would rather introduce renewal to the parent church. Luther was a devout monk who longed to reform the Catholic Church, not start another. Wesley never left the Anglican Church (although often denied a pulpit) and kept the growing Methodist Movement within the Church of England during his lifetime. Another Methodist, Benjamin T. Roberts, started the Free Methodist Church only as a last resort, having been denied a voice in his own denomination, and only then at the initiative of others who had been expelled from the Methodist Church.

Numerous other examples could be listed. In many cases schism could have been avoided and parent churches enriched if only those churches had welcomed with open arms the fellowship and the practice of the gifts of grace of their Charismatic brothers and sisters. We have known several churches in our own experience where this has happened, and in fact "Charismatic" and "noncharismatic" believers (in the popular sense of the term) coexist peaceably and supportively in many evangelical churches today. In failing to show this flexibility, churches have often lost the opportunity to guide renewal groups into broader maturity and usefulness.[5]

CONCLUSION

Contemporary Wesleyans may be uniquely placed to be God's instrument for a new and dynamic outbreak of the gospel in our day. We are rooted in the best of the catholic, evangelical, and charismatic traditions. Perhaps we can learn, like Wesley, to be that "wise householder who can produce from his store both the new and the old" (Matt. 13:52 PHILLIPS). Jeremy Rifkin, in his book *The Emerging Order*, asserts,

> If the Charismatic and evangelical strains of the new Christian renewal movement [today] come together and unite a liberating energy with a new covenant vision for society, it is possible that a great religious awakening will take place, one potentially powerful enough to incite a second Protestant reformation.
>
> It is also possible that as the domestic and global situation continues to worsen . . . the evangelical/Charismatic phenomena, and the waves of religious renewal that follow, could, instead, provide a growing sanctuary for millions of frightened Americans and even a recruiting ground for a repressive movement manifesting all of the earmarks of an emerging fascism.[6]

Wesleyanism already bridges the evangelical and Charismatic camps to some degree today. It has a clear message of present deliverance from inbred sin by the power of the sanctifying Spirit. If it needs anything, it is a new infusion of and openness to the power of the Holy Spirit and a new appreciation for the breadth and balance of its own heritage as seen in John Wesley himself.

A GUIDE TO USING SPIRITUAL GIFTS

God wants the church to be the *visible* Body of Christ in today's world. He calls us to continue the ministry begun on earth by Jesus Christ, based on our total faith in him and the free work of the Holy Spirit in us, the believing community.

One key to God's work in the church is good stewardship of the various gifts of the Spirit. The apostle Paul says, "There are different kinds of gifts, but the same Spirit. . . . Now to each one the manifestation of the Spirit is given for the common good" (1 Cor. 12:4,7). And the apostle Peter says, "Each one should use whatever gift he has received to serve others, faithfully administering [or being a good steward of] God's grace in its various forms" (1 Peter 4:10).

The following pages outline the biblical teaching on spiritual gifts and show how gifts fit in the life of the church. We will see what it means in practice for us as believers to be united together in one Body.

Key Scriptures: Romans 12:4–8; 1 Corinthians 12–14; Ephesians 4:11–16; Hebrews 2:4; 1 Peter 4:10–11.

Supplemental Scriptures: Romans 1:11; 1 Corinthians 1:7; 7:7; 1 Timothy 4:14; 2 Timothy 1:6; Exodus 35:30–35.

Definition: A spiritual gift is God's grace working through the personality of the believer, equipping him or her for particular ministry, so that the church may be strengthened in worship, fellowship, and witness. Thus the kingdom of God is advanced and God is glorified in all things.

PRINCIPLES RELATING TO SPIRITUAL GIFTS

The biblical teaching on the gifts of the Spirit can be summarized in ten major points. Following these points we suggest seven steps for helping believers discover their gifts.

1. *Gifts are given for the proper functioning of the church in all ages—for its edification, integrity, and wholeness.* The constant concern of the New Testament writers is that the church may be "edified," or built up. It is the whole body, not just individual believers, which is to "become mature, attaining to the whole measure of the fullness of Christ" (Eph. 4:13). Paul shows in Ephesians 4 that the church "builds itself up in love" through the ministry of each believer, "as each part does its work" (v. 16). Understanding, discovering, and exercising gifts is a basic part of this maturing process.

The Bible tells us that the "fullness" of God's grace is found in Jesus Christ (Col. 1:19). From this fullness God the Spirit distributes gifts to each believer (Eph. 4:7) so that we may live, love, and serve as Jesus did. This is what it means to be the Body of Christ.

2. *Every believer has at least one spiritual gift.* The New Testament writers waste no time trying to prove this point, for in the early church the universal distribution of gifts to all believers was assumed and understood. Paul says, "To *each one* the manifestation of the Spirit is given" (1 Cor. 12:7).

That every believer has at least one gift is confirmed by the fact that we are all members of each other (Rom. 12:5). To be a part of the body is to have a function in the body, for no part of the body is useless or unnecessary. Part of spiritual growth is discovering just where we fit in the body. This is where spiritual gifts come in.

3. *No believer has all the gifts.* How easily we assume that pastors or other leaders should have all the spiritual gifts! Yet the Bible nowhere promises this. We expect too much if we think a pastor can teach, counsel, administer, organize, evangelize, and disciple others. Rather each person, including leaders, is to function according to the grace God has given him or her.

Only one person in history had all the gifts, and that is our Head, Jesus Christ. The Bible specifically tells us that Jesus was an apostle, prophet, teacher, healer, and miracle worker. Whether he ever spoke in tongues we do not know; the New Testament is silent. As our Head and Leader, and the source of our own ministries, Jesus distributes grace gifts to each of us so that we may *together* be able to continue his kingdom ministry on earth. The point of the gifts, however, is precisely that the gifts are *distributed.* The church is a body, not one gigantic arm or mouth. Paul says, "If the whole body were an eye, where would the sense of hearing be?" (1 Cor. 12:17). Our goal should be to find our own gifts and help equip others to exercise theirs—not seek to have all the gifts ourselves.

4. *No single gift should be expected or required of all believers.* This also follows from the fact that we together all make up the Body of Christ. How absurd to require, for example, that every believer should be a mouth or a foot! This is part of what Paul is teaching the Corinthians. They were exalting some gifts over others and competing in gifts to demonstrate their supposed spirituality. Paul calls them to account, downplaying the very gifts they were most excited about.

Perhaps we have heard persons especially gifted in evangelism or in intercessory prayer tell of their ministry and encourage others to imitate them. We must be careful about this. We can rejoice in every believer's ministry, but not everyone is gifted as an evangelist or called to a special prayer ministry. Every believer is to pray and to be a witness, but we will vary greatly in the way we do this, partly according to our gifts. Likewise with speaking in tongues. God gives some this gift, not all, as he sovereignly chooses. We should neither expect all believers to speak in tongues, even when they are filled with the Spirit, nor forbid this gift when God does give it.

5. *Gifts are usually related to our personalities.* Often we can see a link between certain personality traits and one's spiritual gifts. Evangelists, for instance, are often people with a natural capacity to meet and influence people. But this is not always the case.

People often ask whether gifts are the same as talents. The biblical answer seems to be that while the two are not the same, yet gifts are often related to or build on talents. For example, a Christian may have a natural ability to teach, but this is not necessarily a spiritual gift. It may become a gift when the person gives himself or herself fully to God and allows the gift to be ignited by the Spirit so that it becomes a genuine channel of God's grace.

We must remember, of course, that even so-called natural abilities already are gifts from God. Paul says in 1 Corinthians 4:7, "What do you have that you did not receive?" Speaking to Jeremiah, God said, "Before I formed you in the womb I knew you, before you were born I set you apart . . . as a prophet to the nations" (Jer. 1:5). God has a plan for each of us. He knows us even before our conception. Now God wishes to use us as we turn over to him all our "natural" abilities and let him make of them what he will. In some cases a connection between these abilities and our gifts is easily recognized; in other cases, perhaps not.

6. *Most spiritual gifts can be counterfeited.* Spiritual gifts are no sure proof of spirituality; one may receive genuine gifts, yet use them improperly. In fact, Paul says the Corinthian church had many gifts but still was carnal, or worldly (1 Cor. 1:7; 3:1–3).

The Bible speaks of false prophets, false apostles (Rev. 2:2), and false teachers. Satan loves to counterfeit gifts and ministries in the church, creating confusion and division. Therefore we need to be on guard against the idea that to be gifted necessarily means to be spiritual. We must avoid any tendency to compare or compete in the matter of gifts.

7. *The gifts of the Spirit are to be accompanied by the fruit of the Spirit* (Gal. 5:22–23). This is the answer to the problem of spiritual counterfeiting. The enemy can counterfeit gifts, but he is unable to counterfeit persuasively, or for very long, the fruit of the Spirit. Love, joy, peace, patience, self-control, and the other fruit of the Spirit *really are* the *fruit* of the Spirit's work in our lives.

Biblically, there is no conflict between the gifts and the fruit of the Spirit, as we saw earlier. Both come from the same source. We should avoid any either/or thinking here—*either* gifts *or* the fruit of the Spirit. The fruit of the Spirit enables us to show the spirit of Jesus Christ; the gifts enable us to minister effectively in Jesus' spirit.

8. *Gifts provide guidance for the church's ministry.* What does God want us to do? What should be the ministry focus of our local church? One way to find out is to look at the gifts God is giving us.

Often churches simply go on year after year with the same ministries, even when the people and gifts in the congregation change. Gifts help us see where our ministry priorities really ought to be. God promises us all the gifts necessary for ministry, so examining the gifts in our congregation may give new clues as to what *God* wants us to do *now*, in the present situation. First, however, we must take care to disciple one another and discover our gifts, for gifts often lie dormant, like dry seeds, awaiting the care and nurture of the congregation and the renewing rain of the Spirit.

9. *Faithfulness in exercising gifts leads to greater fruitfulness.* Jesus teaches this in his parables. The faithful steward of God's grace is given still more. Jesus says, "This is to my Father's glory, that you bear much fruit, showing yourselves to be my disciples" (John 15:8).

This is a crucial aspect of spiritual stewardship and growth. Perhaps the most important church growth we can hope and pray for is growth in gift ministry in the spirit of Jesus. For that will surely lead to the growth of the body in numbers as well as in Christlikeness. In this sense, our most important stewardship is the stewardship of God's grace gifts to us.

10. *The equipping gifts* (apostle, prophet, evangelist, pastor, teacher) *are given so all believers may be enabled to use their gifts in Christian ministry.* The New Testament makes this clear in Ephesians 4:11–12, a key text for understanding ministry and leadership in the Bible. God gives "apostles, prophets, evangelists, pastors, and teachers" to the church precisely "to prepare God's people for works of service," or "for the work of ministry." The key role of pastoral leaders in the church is equipping all believers for ministry. If we compare Ephesians 4:11–12 with 1 Corinthians 12:28, we see that this equipping involves, among other things, helping each person to discover and use his or her gifts.

Significantly, the New Testament presents no hierarchy of leaders in the church. It does not distinguish between those who are ministers and those who are not, for we are all called to ministry. Rather, the New Testament shows that precisely because all are gifted, some receive equipping or enabling gifts (leadership gifts) to help the whole body become a ministering community. This is the key to gifts becoming not simply disconnected appendages but part of the effective functioning of the whole body. In this way gifts really become practical and strategic in the overall life and ministry of the church.

DISCOVERING OUR GIFTS

These guidelines for understanding gifts lead naturally to an important question: How can I discover my spiritual gift? Or, better, how can my church discover and use God's gifts effectively? We suggest seven steps:

1. *Live in total obedience to God.* Gifts can become a trap or a detour from spiritual maturity for people who are fighting God at some point in their lives. The first step for all of us is to seek the Giver, not the gift. Only when we have determined to obey God in everything are we ready to turn our attention to gifts. If church members are already exercising gifts, they must be careful to keep obeying God in all areas of life. This is the insurance against spiritual counterfeits.

2. *Know about gifts and how they function in the church.* Nothing substitutes for sound biblical knowledge about gifts. Teaching on gifts and how they function in the normal life and ministry of the church is an essential ingredient in effective discipling.

3. *Participate in small-group Bible study.* This is perhaps the best way to learn about gifts, for in small groups learning is linked to growth in fellowship, caring, and ministry to one another. This was part of the genius of the Methodist bands and class meetings.

A good approach is to join with a dozen or so other

people in studying the biblical material on gifts. But this should be done in connection with a broader study of the church in the New Testament. A combined study of Ephesians, Hebrews, 1 Corinthians 12–14, and Romans 12–15 may be useful. The group might also want to use some good books on gifts, such as Kenneth Kinghorn's *Gifts of the Spirit*. Prayer for one another, and for each other's gifts and ministries, should be a natural part of this group experience.

4. *Examine your aspirations for ministry and service.* What do you dream of doing for God? How would you really like to minister? These dreams and aspirations may give clues to undeveloped areas of giftedness in your life. Make this a careful matter of prayer. Keeping a spiritual journal may help. Morton Kelsey's *Adventure Inward: Christian Growth Through Personal Journal Writing* (Minneapolis: Augsburg, 1980) is a useful resource for this kind of enterprise.

5. *Experiment with different kinds of ministry.* It may take time to discover your gifts. But simply finding places to serve others will help. As you practice servanthood in the spirit of Jesus, you may find areas of ministry you never dreamed of.

As we learn more about ourselves and our gifts, we will know better when to say yes and when to say no to ministry opportunities. In the meantime, we should simply seek to be servants. Regardless of where our gifts lie, the overriding quality of our lives should be serving one another in love (Gal. 5:13).

6. *Evaluate results and reactions.* How did you feel about your service to others, and what was the result? How did others respond? Here also we may find clues to giftedness.

As we begin to discover gift areas in our lives, we will sense the fulfillment of being used of God. We will find

ourselves discovering new identities as Christian work-
ers. We will find that God is working both through us and
in us, and that the results are more than could be
expected from a merely human standpoint.

7. *Expect the confirmation of the church.* Here is a
safeguard against any "Lone Ranger" attitude toward
gifts. We don't discover gifts by going off in a corner by
ourselves, and we don't exercise our gifts all by ourselves.
Our gift ministry is part of our contribution to the Body.
As we minister in the spirit of Jesus, God through his
people will confirm and encourage our gifts.

Gifts may be recognized and confirmed in many
ways. Ordination to pastoral leadership is one way the
church affirms God's gifts for ministry. Each church
should find appropriate ways to recognize and affirm
members' gifts in many areas, from evangelism to discipling to hospitality to administration.

This means, of course, that our lives must be lived in
intimate union with our sisters and brothers in the
Christian community. As love, trust, and encouragement
increase, the church will joyfully confirm our gifts.
Moreover, it will find ways to encourage and support us
in our gifts so that our ministry may grow and the whole
church benefit.

What is the result of all this? "Then we will no longer
be infants, tossed back and forth by the waves, and blown
here and there by every kind of teaching and by the
cunning and craftiness of men in their deceitful scheming.
Instead, speaking the truth in love, we will in all things
grow up into him who is the Head, that is, Christ. From
him the whole body, joined and held together by every
supporting ligament, grows and builds itself up in love,
as each part does its work" (Eph. 4:14-16).

Here is God's description of a church that is both holy
and charismatic.

NOTES

CHAPTER ONE

[1] W.T Purkiser, *The Gifts of the Spirit* (Kansas City, Mo.: Beacon Hill Press, 1975), p. 17.

[2] See the helpful discussion in John Howard Yoder, "The Fullness of Christ: Perspectives on Ministries in Renewal," *Concern* 17 (February 1969): 63–64. For a discussion of "charismatic fullness" as this term was used by Daniel Steele, see Delbert R. Rose, "Distinguishing Things that Differ," *Wesleyan Theological Journal* 9 (Spring 1974): 8–11.

[3] Note also Philippians 2:9; Colossians 2:23; 2 Corinthians 2:10 and 12:13; Ephesians 4:32. The fact that *charidzomai* can also be translated "forgive" (as in the last passage) further underscores the essential nature of this emphasis and its ecclesiological importance.

[48] See Jaroslav Pelikan, *Spirit Versus Structure* (New York: Harper and Row, 1968).

CHAPTER TWO

[1] John T. Nichol, *Pentecostalism* (New York: Harper and Row, 1966), p. 19.

[2] Evelyn Underhill, *Worship* (New York: Harper and Row, 1936), pp. 236–37.

[3] Morton T. Kelsey, *Tongue Speaking: An Experiment in Spiritual Experience* (New York: Doubleday, 1964), p. 33.

[4] Joseph W. Trigg, "The Charismatic Intellectual: Origen's Understanding of Religious Leadership," *Church History* (March 1981): 12–13.

[5] Origen, *Homilies on Numbers* 22.4 (7.209.3-14), quoted by Trigg, pp. 13–14.

[6] See Trigg, pp. 14–19.

[7] Kenneth Scott Latourette, *A History of Christianity* (New York: Harper and Brothers, 1953), p. 130.

[8] Ibid.

[9] Ibid., p. 132.

[10] See R. Leonard Carroll, "Glossolalia: Apostles to the Reformation," *The Glossolalia Phenomenon,* ed. Wade H. Horton (Cleveland, Tenn.: Pathway Press, 1966), pp. 67-94.

[11] Robert M. Anderson, *Vision of the Disinherited* (New York: Oxford University Press, 1979), p. 25.

[12] Richard Quebedeaux, *The New Charismatics* (New York: Doubleday, 1976), pp. 20–21.

[13] Ibid., p. 21.

[14] Augustine, *On the Gospel of John*, Tractate 32, in Philip Schaff, ed., *Nicene and Post-Nicene Fathers of the Christian Church*, 1st series (Grand Rapids: Eerdmans, 1974 repr.), 7:195.

[15] Vinson Synan, *In the Latter Days: The Outpouring of the Holy Spirit in the Twentieth Century* (Ann Arbor: Servant Books, 1984), p. 29.

[16] See Latourette, p. 155, for a copy of the original Nicene Creed. The full classical doctrine of the Holy Spirit as the Third Person of the Trinity emerges only with Augustine.

[17] Latourette, p. 164.

[18] Kelsey, p. 42.

[19] Ibid., p. 43.

[20] E. Glenn Hinson, "A Brief History of Glossolalia," in Frank Stagg, E. Glenn Hinson, and Wayne E. Oates, *Glossolalia: Tongue Speaking in Biblical, Historical, and Psychological Perspective* (Nashville: Abingdon, 1967), p. 58.

[21] Latourette, p. 453.

[22] See Louis Bouyer, "Some Charismatic Movements in the History of the Church," in Edward D. O'Connor, ed., *Perspectives on Charismatic Renewal* (Notre Dame, Ind.: University of Notre Dame Press, 1975). Bouyer writes, ". . . there is no doubt that early monasticism . . . was in its origins a definitely charismatic movement" (p. 120).

[23] Hinson writes, "New sects have resulted as frequently from the unwillingness of the majority to accept the minority as from undue pride or inherent factional tendencies among the spiritualists. So many factors can and have contributed to divisions within Christendom that it would not be fair to these movements to single them out for censure" (p. 74).

[24] Kenneth C. Kinghorn, *Gifts of the Spirit* (Nashville: Abingdon, 1976), p. 15.

[25] *Sermons on the First Epistle of St. Peter*, Luther's Works 30, pp. 123–24.

[26] Ibid., pp. 124–25.

[27] *Commentary on Psalm 110*, Luther's Works 13, p. 332.

[28] Ibid., pp. 294–95.

[29] In *Concerning Ministry* Luther speaks of "the office of teachers, prophets, governing, speaking with tongues, the gifts of healing and helping, as Paul directs in 1 Cor. 12" (Luther's Works 40, p. 36).

[30] Kinghorn, p. 16.

[31] John Calvin, *The Epistles of Paul the Apostle to the Galatians, Ephesians, Philippians and Colossians* (Grand Rapids: Eerdmans, 1965), p. 178.

[32] Ibid.

[33] Kinghorn, p. 17.

[34] Synan, *In the Latter Days*, p. 29.

[35] Quebedeaux, p. 21.

[36] Ibid., p. 22.

[37] Ibid., p. 21.

[38] Ibid.

[39] Synan, *In the Latter Days*, p. 32–35. Also see P. E. Shaw, *The Catholic Apostolic Church* (New York: King's Crown, 1946), and Andrew L. Drummond, *Edward Irving and His Circle* (London: James Clark and Co., 1935).

[40] Anderson, pp. 26–27.

[41] Quebedeaux, pp. 22–23.

[42] George Carey, *A Tale of Two Churches* (Downers Grove, Ill.: InterVarsity Press, 1985), p. 17.

CHAPTER THREE

[1]For an informative discussion of second-experience theology and its significance to Pentecostalism see Charles E. Hummel, *Fire in the Fireplace: Contemporary Charismatic Renewal* (Downers Grove, Ill.: InterVarsity Press, 1978), pp. 54–62. Also see the chapter below, "What Happened to the Holiness Movement?" (The Pilgrim Holiness Church merged with the Wesleyan Methodist Church in 1966 to form the Wesleyan Church.)

[2]For an overview of religious developments in this period see Vinson Synan, *The Holiness-Pentecostal Movement in the United States* (Grand Rapids: Eerdmans, 1971), pp. 57–76, 95–116.

[3]Ibid., pp. 99–103.

[4]Ibid., pp. 103–116.

[5]Condensed from the *Los Angeles Times* (April 18, 1906): 1.

[6]Synan, *The Holiness-Pentecostal Movement*, p. 124.

[7]Hummel, pp. 43–44.

[8]Ibid., pp. 44–45.

[9]Ibid., pp. 19–28.

[10]For a summary of the ministry of Oral Roberts see Steve Durasoff, *Bright Wind of the Spirit* (Englewood Cliffs, N.J.: Prentice-Hall, 1972), pp. 131–44.

[11]Hummel, pp. 17–18.

[12]Durasoff, p. 150. For a full history of the FGBMFI see Durasoff, pp. 145–165.

[13]Synan, *In the Latter Days*, pp. 132–33.

[14]H. M. Carson, "Roman Catholicism," in *The New International Dictionary of the Christian Church*, ed. J. D. Douglas, rev. ed. (Grand Rapids: Zondervan, 1978), p. 855.

[15]See Synan, *In the Latter Days*, pp. 98–100; also Leon Joseph Cardinal Suenens, *A New Pentecost?*, trans. Francis Martin (New York: Seabury, 1975).

[16]Synan, *In the Latter Days*, p. 108.

[17]Bouyer has comments that are relevant to the contemporary movement and the historical perspective traced in chapter 2. He writes, "Is the Pentecostal movement something as new in the Catholic Church as it seems to many people? . . . [Historical examples] show that such movements are a quasi-permanent or ever-recurrent, feature of the life of the Catholic Church" (p. 113). Further, Bouyer writes, "The Pentecostal manifestations of the Spirit . . . have never truly ceased within the Catholic (or Orthodox) Church. From the very beginning, as we can see in the case of the Corinthians, they have always been in some danger of falling into schism or heresy but have never for that reason been condemned as wrong in principle, either by the greatest spiritual theologians or by the Church authorities" (p. 129).

[18]See Kevin and Dorothy Ranaghan, *The Catholic Pentecostal Movement* (Paramus, N.J., 1969), pp. 6–16.

[19]See Synan, *In the Latter Days*, pp. 111–17.

[20]Carson, p. 856.

[21]Synan, *In the Latter Days*, p. 119.

[22]Ibid., pp. 53–54.

[23]Ibid., p. 13.

[24]Ibid.

[25]Ibid., p. 65.

[26]Ibid., p. 16.

[27]Ibid., p. 7.

[28]Quebedeaux, p. 145.

[29]James D. G. Dunn, *Jesus and the Spirit* (London: SCM Press, 1975), p. 341.

[30]Kinghorn, *Gifts of the Spirit*, pp. 122–23.

[31]Jürgen Moltmann, *The Church in the Power of the Spirit*, trans. Margaret Kohl (New York: Harper and Row, 1977), p. 10.

[32]Hans Küng, "The Charismatic Structure of the Church," in Hans Küng, ed., *The Church and Ecumenism*, Vol. 4 of *Concilium* (New York: Paulist Press, 1965), p. 49. See also Küng, *The Church* (Garden City, N.J.: Doubleday Image, 1976), especially pp. 236–50.

[33]Küng, "The Charismatic Structure of the Church," pp. 50–58.

[34]Ibid., p. 54.

[35]Ibid., p. 58.

[36]Ibid.

[37]John Wesley, "Upon Our Lord's Sermon on the Mount," Discourse IV, *The Works of the Rev. John Wesley*, ed. Frank Baker, Vol. 1, *Sermons*, ed. Albert C. Outler (Nashville: Abingdon Press, 1984), p. 533.

CHAPTER FOUR

[1]It has occasionally been argued that Wesley himself spoke in tongues, but we have found no solid evidence for this claim.

[2]Sermon, "The Good Steward," *The Works of John Wesley*, 3rd ed., ed. Thomas Jackson (14 vols; London, 1829–1831; variously reprinted), 6:147. Hereafter cited as *Works* (Jackson).

[3]Colin W. Williams, *John Wesley's Theology Today* (New York: Abingdon Press, 1960), p. 44.

[4]Sermon, "On Working Out Our Own Salvation," *Works* (Jackson), 6:512. Thus it is a distortion of Wesley to say, as some critics have, that Wesley held that a person could turn to God purely on his own, without the operation of the grace of God.

[5]*Explanatory Notes on the New Testament* (London: Epworth Press, 1958), p. 411.

[6]*Works* (Jackson), 10:82.

[7]Sermon, "Of the Church," *Works* (Jackson), 6:397. By "wrong opinions" Wesley meant even wrong or faulty doctrine.

[8]Albert C. Outler in Dow Kirkpatrick, ed., *The Doctrine of the Church* (New York: Abingdon, 1964), p. 19.

[9]Sermon, "Scriptural Christianity," *Works* (Jackson), 5:38.

[10]*Explanatory Notes*, p. 625 (1 Cor. 12:31). Note his comment on healing, p. 623.

[11]Ibid., pp. 713, 628 (Eph. 4:12; 1 Cor. 14:5).

[12]Ibid. See also Sermon, "The More Excellent Way," *Works* (Jackson), 7:27; *Explanatory Notes*, p. 713 (on Eph. 4:8–11).

[13]It has been suggested that Wesley's use of the term "extraordinary" is to be understood in contradistinction to the eighteenth-century ecclesiastical meaning of "ordinary," so that it would mean, in effect, "outside the normal ordained ministry" in a more or less technical sense. A search of several dictionaries does not bear this out, however. Even in Wesley's day "extraordinary" had the common sense meaning of simply "outside of what is ordinary or usual" (*Oxford English Dictionary*, 3:468,472). Thus a 1706 London dictionary defines extraordinary as "beyond or contrary to common Order and Fashion, unusual, uncommon," and a dictionary published in London in 1790 has

"Different from common order and method; eminent, remarkable, more than common." It appears that Wesley was using the term in the general and popular sense, not as a technical ecclesiastical designation. (This is underscored by the fact that Wesley seems to use "extraordinary" synonymously with "miraculous" when referring to the gifts.)

[14] *Works* (Jackson), 7:27.

[15] *Works* (Jackson), 5:38. Behind this distinction is a practical issue of ecclesiology: He was seeking to justify biblically his use of "lay" preachers as "extraordinary" ministers parallel to the prophets and evangelists of the New Testament. See Howard A. Snyder, *The Radical Wesley and Patterns for Church Renewal* (Downers Grove, Ill.: InterVarsity Press, 1980), pp. 90–102.

[16] *Works* (Jackson), 7:26–27.

[17] *Works* (Jackson), 5:38. The idea of the "restitution of all things" (cf. Acts 3:21) is important for Wesley's theology and ties in with some Charismatic themes.

[18] *The Journal of John Wesley, A. M.,* ed. Nehemiah Curnock (London: Epworth Press, 1938), 2:136–37.

[19] *Explanatory Notes,* p. 631 (a comment not found in Bengel).

[20] Letter to the Reverend Dr. Conyers Middleton, *Works* (Jackson), 10:56.

[21] *Explanatory Notes,* pp. 629, 631 (1 Cor. 14:15, 28). Here again Wesley inserts his own comment, not following Bengel.

[22] See, among others, Kelsey, pp. 54–55; also George Barton Cutten, *Speaking With Tongues Historically and Psychologically Considered* (New Haven: Yale University Press, 1927), pp. 48–66. Both Kelsey and Cutten refer to Wesley in this regard.

[23] Albert C. Outler, "John Wesley as Theologian—Then and Now," *Methodist History* 12:4 (July 1974): 79.

[24] *Explanatory Notes,* p. 884.

[25] See Wesley's "Farther Appeal to Men of Reason and Religion," I, Section V, in *The Works of John Wesley,* ed. Frank Baker, Vol. 11 (New York: Oxford University Press, 1975), pp. 138–76.

[26] *Works* (Jackson), 14:320–21.

[27] Ibid. See also Wesley's fourth sermon on the Sermon on the Mount, in *Works,* ed. Baker, 1:533–34, where he speaks of Christianity as "essentially a social religion."

[28] "A Plain Account of the People Called Methodists," *Works* (Jackson), 8:251–52.

[29] Franklin Littell, "Class Meeting," *World Parish* 9 (February 1961): 15.

[30] Williams, pp. 151, 150.

[31] This is discussed in greater length in Howard Snyder's book *The Radical Wesley and Patterns for Church Renewal.*

[32] "A Plain Account of the People Called Methodists," *Works* (Jackson), 8:261.

[33] David du Plessis in Theodore Runyon, ed., *What the Spirit Is Saying to the Churches* (New York: Hawthorn Books, 1975), p. 99.

CHAPTER FIVE

[1] For the historical development of Wesley's views on sanctification, see John Leland Peters, *Christian Perfectionism and American Methodism* (Nashville: Abington, 1956).

²For an overview of the Holiness Movement, see Melvin Dieter, *The Holiness Revival of the Nineteenth Century* (Metuchen, N.J.: Scarecrow Press, 1980).

³Dieter, p. 47.

⁴On the decline of the class meeting, see especially Samuel Emerick, ed., *Spiritual Renewal for Methodism: A Discussion of the Early Methodist Class Meeting and the Values Inherent in Personal Groups Today* (Nashville: Methodist Evangelistic Materials, 1958), particularly the chapters by Mary Alice Tenney, Robert Chiles, and J. A. Leatherman; and Luke L. Keefer, Jr., "The Class Meeting's Role of Discipline in Methodism" (unpublished manuscript, 1974).

⁵Charles W. Ferguson, *Organizing to Beat the Devil: Methodists and the Making of America* (Garden City, N.Y.: Doubleday, 1971), p. 149.

⁶Seth C. Rees, *The Ideal Pentecostal Church* (Cincinnati: M. W. Knapp, The Revivalist Office, 1897), p. 13.

⁷Some significant work on this tendency has been done by several Wesleyan scholars. Note especially Donald W. Dayton, "From Christian Perfection to the 'Baptism of the Holy Ghost,'" and Melvin E. Dieter, "Wesleyan-Holiness Aspects of Pentecostal Origins," both in Vinson Synan, *Aspects of Pentecostal-Charismatic Origins* (Plainfield, N.J.: Logos International, 1975), pp. 39–54 and 55–80.

⁸Dieter in Synan, *Aspects of Pentecostal-Charismatic Origins*, p. 62.

⁹Note in Rees the use of such phrases as "Pentecostal fire," "Pentecostal electrocution," "dynamite," "jagged bolts of Pentecostal lightning," "condensed lightning from the upper skies," etc. (Rees, *passim*).

¹⁰Holiness losses to Pentecostalism seem to have been significant in the early years. See Dieter, "Wesleyan-Holiness Aspects of Pentecostal Origins," p. 75.

¹¹Synan, *In the Latter Days*, p. 125.

¹²Terry D. Bilhartz, *Francis Asbury's America* (Grand Rapids: Zondervan, 1984), p. 45.

CHAPTER SIX

¹See, for example, Harvey J. S. Blaney, "St. Paul's Posture on Speaking in Unknown Tongues," *Wesleyan Theological Journal* 8 (Spring 1973): 52–60; Charles D. Isbell, "Glossolalia and Propheteialalia: A Study in I Corinthians 14," *WTJ* 10 (Spring 1975): 15–22; Charles W. Carter, "A Wesleyan View of the Spirit's Gift of Tongues in the Book of Acts," *WTJ* 4 (Spring 1969): 39–68; Carter, *The Person and Ministry of the Holy Spirit: A Wesleyan Perspective* (Grand Rapids: Baker, 1974, 1977), especially pp. 181–220; Carter, introduction and notes on 1 Corinthians in *The Wesleyan Bible Commentary*, ed. Charles W. Carter (Grand Rapids: Eerdmans, 1965), especially 5:114–16, 197–208, 214–23; LLoyd H. Knox, *Key Biblical Perspectives on Tongues* (Winona Lake, Ind.: Light and Life Press, 1974); Wesley L. Duewel, *The Holy Spirit and Tongues* (Winona Lake, Ind.: Light and Life Press, 1974). Most of these employ similar arguments, although the contrasting treatment of just what Paul means by "tongues" in 1 Corinthians 14 reveals the difficulty of basing a total prohibition of glossolalia on the New Testament material.

²Hummel, p. 203.

³Ibid.

⁴Knox, p. 18.

⁵Blaney, p. 55.

[6]Knox, pp. 16ff.; Duewel, p. 21.

[7]Timothy Smith sees this as the most foundational argument against tongues, as do many others. Timothy L. Smith, *Speaking the Truth in Love: Some Honest Questions for Pentecostals* (Kansas City, Mo.: Beacon Hill Press, 1977), pp. 42–47. It is not helpful to cite Wesley here, because he never faced the modern phenomenon of glossolalia.

[8]Hummel tentatively suggests four possible purposes for tongues-speaking, pp. 203–4. See also Kelsey, pp. 218–33.

[9]Hummel, p. 135.

[10]Frank Carver notes that "apart from those who have a pro- or con-tongues axe to grind for ecclesiastical reasons the tongues in 1 Corinthians 14 is normally judged" by New Testament scholarship "to be some form of ecstatic utterance" (Carver, p. 13).

[11]Hummel, p. 158.

[12]"A Colloquy on the Loss and Recovery of the Sacred," sponsored by the evangelically-Methodist-oriented Fund for Theological Education, November 5–9, 1979, at the University of Notre Dame, and a subsequent similar conference on the hallowing of life, included a range of both Wesleyan and Charismatic scholars.

[13]See, for example, E. Stanley Jones, *The Christ of the Mount* (New York: Abingdon-Cokesbury, 1931) and *Is the Kingdom of God Realism?* (New York: Abingdon-Cokesbury, 1940).

[14]Sermon, "Catholic Spirit," *Works* (Jackson), 5:492–504.

CHAPTER SEVEN

[1]See Synan, *In the Latter Days*, pp. 83–86.

[2]See Quebedeaux, pp. 166–74.

[3]*The Charismatic Movement in the Lutheran Church in America: A Pastoral Perspective* (New York: LCA, 1974).

[4]*The Person and Work of the Holy Spirit* (Oklahoma City: Presbyterian Charismatic Communion, 1971).

[5]United Presbyterian Church, U.S.A., *The Work of the Holy Spirit* (Philadelphia: UPCUSA, 1970).

[6]Quebedeaux, p. 164.

[7]United Presbyterian Church, U.S.A., p. 23.

[8]Kilian McDonnell, "Catholic Pentecostalism: Problems in Evaluation," *Dialog* (Winter 1970): 54.

[9]"Tongues: Updating Some Old Issues," Editorial, *Eternity* (March 1973): 8.

[10]"The Gift of Tongues," Editorial, *Christianity Today* (April 11, 1969),: 27–28.

[11]Synan, *In the Latter Days*, p. 137, quoted from Harold Lindsell, *The Holy Spirit in the Latter Days* (Nashville: Thomas Nelson, 1983).

[12]Synan, *In the Latter Days*, p. 124.

[13]John R. W. Stott, *The Baptism and Fullness of the Holy Spirit* (Downers Grove, Ill.: InterVarsity Press, 1964), p. 59.

[14]Quoted in Synan, *In the Latter Days*, pp. 136–37, from *Pastoral Renewal* VIII, no. 1 (July–August 1983): 3–4. By "in a congregational way" Wagner apparently means incorporating gifts without any major change in doctrine or polity.

[15]George Carey, p. 17.

[16]Ibid.

CHAPTER EIGHT

[1] Wayne Oates in Runyon, *What the Spirit Is Saying to the Churches*, p. 83.

[2] See Stephen B. Clark, *Unordained Elders and Renewal Communities* (New York: Paulist Press, 1976), pp. 2–3; and Donald Durnbaugh, *The Believers Church: The History and Character of Radical Protestantism* (New York: Macmillan, 1968).

[3] Clark, pp. 3–4.

[4] Ibid., p. 8.

[5] See the discussion of the contrasting "charismatic" and "institutional" views on renewal in Howard Snyder, *The Radical Wesley*, pp. 125–42.

[6] Jeremy Rifkin, *The Emerging Order: God in the Age of Scarcity* (New York: G. P. Putnam's Sons, 1979), p. xi.

INDEX

Anabaptists, 33f.
Anderson, Robert, 36, 109, 110
Anglican Church. *See* Church of England
Apostles, 24, 32, 102, 105
Apostleship, 14, 57; and community, 17
Arianism, 25
Asbury, Francis, 75
Asbury, Richard, 40f.
Ascetic Movement, 95, 97
Assemblies of God, 48
Atonement, 55
Augustine, 26f., 110
Azusa Street Revival, 40–42

Bands, 63, 66
Baxter, Ern, 85
Bengel, J. A., 61
Bennett, Dennis, 42f.
Bilharz, Terry D., 114
Bishops, 24, 75
Blaney, Harvey J., 114
Bouyer, Louis, 110–11
Buskirk, Jimmy, 91

Calvin, John, 31, 32f.; on spiritual gifts, 32f.
Camp meetings, 69f.
Campbell, Mary, 35
Carey, George, 37, 93, 110, 116
Carlyle, Thomas, 35
Carroll, R. Leonard, 109
Carson, H. M., 111
Carter, Charles W., 114
Carver, Frank, 115
Cashwell, G. B., 41f.
Charismata, charismatic gifts. *See* Gifts of the Spirit

Charismatic Movement, 7ff., 11f., 17, 34, 39, 64ff., 68, 73f., 84f., 88–93, 96–99; among Evangelicals, 44; and church growth, 47f.; compared with Pentecostalism, 48f., 84f.; diversity in, 48f.; history of, 42–49; in Roman Catholicism, 45–47; statistics of, 47f.
Charismatic leader, 11
Charismatic: meaning of term, 77, 11ff.
Charismatic Renewal: in Roman Catholicism, 42, 64ff., 74, 84–85, 96f.
Chiles, Robert, 114
Christ: fullness of, 52, 71, 101, 109
Christian perfection. *See* Sanctification
Christianity Today magazine, 90
Christology, 48
Chrysostom, 26f.
Church of the Nazarene, 39, 40, 74
Church of England, 64, 66, 98
Church, 100; as catholic, 25, 56; as charismatic, 8f., 11–17, 45f., 49–53, 55ff., 64, 74, 86f.; as community, 15, 16f., 52, 86, 100; as holy, 50, 56, 74, 108; as institution, 17, 23, 45f., 49, 57, 64, 65, 86; as organism, 16, 45f., 86; gifts in, 14f., 19ff., 90; in history, 19ff.; in the New Testament, 22, 55f.; structure of, 17, 22f., 52
Clark, Stephen, 97, 116
Class meeting, 63f., 66, 69f., 72, 86, 98, 114
Cluniac reforms, 95
Community, 15, 16f., 52, 69f.; and gifts, 15, 62; and sanctification, 15; church as, 52, 62f., 86; structures for, 69f.
Constantine, 25, 59